My War against the Nazis

My War against the Nazis
A Jewish Soldier with the Red Army

ADAM BRONER

Foreword by Antony Polonsky

THE UNIVERSITY OF ALABAMA PRESS
Tuscaloosa

Typeface is Minion

∞

The paper on which this book is printed meets the minimum requirements of American National Standard for Information Sciences-Permanence of Paper for Printed Library Materials, ANSI Z39.48-1984.

Library of Congress Cataloging-in-Publication Data

Broner, Adam, 1925–
    My war against the Nazis : a Jewish soldier with the Red Army / Adam Broner ; foreword by Antony Polonsky.
        p.   cm. — (Fire ant books)
    Includes bibliographical references and index.
    ISBN-13: 978-0-8173-5417-6 (pbk. : alk. paper)
    ISBN-10: 0-8173-5417-4 (pbk. : alk. paper)
    1. Broner, Adam, 1925– 2. World War, 1939–1945—Participation, Jewish. 3. World War, 1939–1945—Personal narratives, Jewish. 4. Soviet Union. Raboche-Krest'ianskaia Krasnaia Armiia—Biography. 5. Poland. Armia—Biography. 6. Jews—Poland—Biography. 7. Jews—Soviet Union—Biography. I. Title.
    D810.J4B75 2007
    940.54′1247092—dc22
    [B]
                                                                    2006028617

To the memory of Barbara's and my parents:
Regina and Abram Holeman
Ajdel Ita and Israel Broner

Contents

Illustrations

Acknowledgments

In the main text of the book I had the difficult task of writing about many perils in my life while here I am pleased to single out only fortunes. First and foremost I am very happy to acknowledge the enormous contribution to this project by my wife, Barbara. On each step of its development Barbara assumed the role of facilitator, advisor, critical reviewer, and technical assistant. Thanks to Barbara's efforts the manuscript moved through several stages of improvement to reach the present form.

The director of the University of Alabama Press recognized the manuscript's potential from its first reading. I am in great debt to him for his supportive enthusiasm, as well as his shepherding of the manuscript to its final form.

Two scholars read the manuscript twice and made very valuable and helpful comments that led to amended contents and improved structure and flow of the narrative. Their repeated recommendations to approve the manuscript for publication are also sincerely appreciated.

Professor Antony Polonsky of Brandeis University lent his prestige to this book by emphasizing its contribution to our understanding of the upheaval and tragedy of World War II. I am appreciative of the time he spent on reading the story of my life and for the kind words expressed in his foreword.

My good friends Dr. Joseph Seneca—longtime chairman of the New Jersey Economic Policy Council—and his lovely spouse, Dr. Rosalind Seneca, spent much time reading an earlier version of the manuscript. They thoroughly analyzed its merits and wrote an insightful commentary, which was very helpful in rethinking many aspects of my evaluation of the drama of my parents and siblings who perished during the Holocaust.

Dr. William Freund—member of the Economic Policy Council for more than twenty years—suggested Sarasota as an ideal place to retire. After fifteen years in retirement we remain close friends with William and his charming wife, Judy, whom we meet often in Sarasota. Not only did Sarasota play an extremely positive role in providing the serene environment for reflexive writing, but it became a place where many of our friends settled as well. Doctors Hanna and Gabriel Temkin; Dr. Jadwiga Brukner and her husband, Morris; Dr. Halina Zawadska and her late husband, Joel Sacks; Rina Eisenberg and her late husband, Eugene Eisenberg; as well as seasonal visitors, the late Nina and Jerry Zachariasz and Luboslawa and Roman Bojmelgrin created a close-knit circle of friends that was intellectually stimulating and helpful in everyday life. Many thanks to all of them!

I am indebted to several readers of my manuscript whose comments were helpful. Among those are Doctors Adele and Fred Bernard. I would also like to thank Norma Adams and Hillel Kuttler for their keen comments and advice on a previous version of this book.

Special thanks to my stepdaughter Eva and her husband, Dr. Roberto Vilarrubi, for their suggestions in the process of fashioning the text. Eva was intrinsically involved in my project, providing editorial comments and advice on how to proceed with its publication.

It was my strong inner feeling to recreate the images of my parents and siblings from memory in order to include them in this book. I considered this my duty and the only means to place tombstones on their unknown resting places. I am grateful to many artists from whom I learned how to paint portraits, including the foremost American portrait artist Daniel Greene, whose printed guides were my teaching adjuncts. Judging from my portraits he may not consider me his student, but I would insist on calling him my teacher, even though we met only once at a demonstration session in Sarasota.

I am most thankful to the managing editor of the University of Alabama Press and to the copy editor Debbie Self for their excellent editorial work and cordial and attentive cooperation with me during this entire process.

Needless to say, all remaining errors of fact or omission are the author's responsibility.

Foreword

The great majority of Jews who survived the Nazi genocide in Poland did so by fleeing to the Soviet Union. This well-written and compelling autobiography is by one such Polish Jew, Adam Broner, who, as a boy of fourteen in November 1939, left his parents and five remaining siblings behind in Lodz, and with his elder brother sought refuge in Bialystok, then under Soviet occupation. He and his brother survived the war but all the rest of his family perished. Broner describes his difficulties in crossing the Soviet frontier and his determination to take part in the war against Hitler, which culminated in his entry into the Polish Army established in the USSR under Communist control in 1943. Broner eventually became a sergeant and participated in the liberation of Poland and the capture of Berlin. But his war, and Poland's, was not over. Broner also participated in the postwar campaigns within liberated Poland, now under Communist control, against the Ukrainian and anticommunist undergrounds.

After demobilization, Broner, committed if not to Communism then at least to the vision of a Poland in which all its citizens, including those of Jewish origin, would be treated as equal, joined the ruling Polish United Workers Party and was trained in Moscow as an economist. In Moscow he met his Russian wife and then returned to Poland, where he obtained an important position in the national financial planning commission. The Polish government's so-called anti-Zionist campaign of 1968, unleashed in the wake of the Israeli victory in the Six Days' War, came as a bitter disillusionment to him and he decided to leave Poland with his wife and children, settling finally in the United States. The account of his life is interspersed with well-drawn and often moving accounts of prewar Jewish life and of remembrances of his family.

This important and moving memoir contributes much to our understanding of the upheaval and tragedy of World War II in Eastern Europe. It also demonstrates yet again how an indomitable human spirit can navigate seemingly impossible circumstances and build a life of meaning and accomplishment.

Antony Polonsky
Brandeis University

Prologue

The train came slowly to a halt. As we were hurried off, I saw that everything was snow covered. I could only manage a quick glimpse to learn where I was. Near the front of the train I noticed a sign that read Kandalaki. I had never heard of it, and it certainly did not appear on the available maps of Siberia. It was clearly much deeper into Siberia than the city of Novosibirsk, where I had been for the last two years. I realized that I was being sent into exile. Was this place part of the Soviet system of gulags? Was I to be one of those destined to forced labor, starvation diets, and a high likelihood of death?

A stranger approached, offering to buy cigarettes. I told him that I had *makhorka,* the dark, chopped leaves of Russian tobacco. He offered to trade a block of chocolate for a cupful of the *makhorka.* The price seemed reasonable, but I wondered how he had chocolate to offer. I asked him naïvely if it was true, as my ten-year-old friend in Lodz had told me, that in Russia children get free chocolate? "Nonsense," the stranger replied with a smile. "We got the chocolate instead of the monthly ration of sugar. Now, in this whole area, everyone has a lot of chocolate and is using it for barter. That's the way our supply system works."

Then, the trader, who must have noticed my accent, asked, "Where are you from?"

"From Poland, now occupied by the Germans."

"How come you are from Poland and wear a Red Army uniform?"

"Well, this is a long story, and I can't tell you now."

"If you are in the Red Army, why are you coming to this coal mine instead of fighting the Germans?"

This guy was getting to the heart of the matter, but I wasn't willing to discuss it with him.

We saw someone approaching and thought it would be better to end this conversation. Hastily, the stranger volunteered the information that work in the nearby coal mine was very difficult, and then he looked at me and said, "You won't last more than three months here." He then disappeared.

In the meantime, the colonel assembled his squad and we were marched to the administration building of the coal mine. Its full name was "Shakhta Kandalaki Trest Molotov Ugol, Kuznietski Bassein." Learning that we had been sent to a coal mine rather than a prison camp eased my apprehension somewhat, but the chocolate trader's revelation had not been encouraging.

After more than two hours the colonel came out from the coal mine office with an order: "*Ryadovoy* Broner is ordered to stay and work in the mine." He announced that several of the other soldiers would be sent to the Soviet Union's new Polish Army. That was outrageous and I was indignant!

My prospects, as revealed to me by the stranger, were very bleak indeed. Actually, it seemed the equivalent of a death sentence. I had not done anything to justify such harsh punishment. I volunteered for the Red Army to join the struggle against the Germans. Did that deserve punishment?

My plan to join an army, which would then liberate Poland and present me with a chance to participate in the rescue of my parents and siblings, was falling apart. Moreover, the likelihood of surviving in the coal mine was close to zero if the trader was to be believed. I could not even hope that Wanda Wasilewska, the Polish Communist and confidant of Stalin and the highest commissars, could get me out from here as the Polish captain had promised; local officials would probably not let me send her a letter.

I decided to appeal to the local military command. The visit to a lieutenant did not help. I argued that I was from Poland, born in the city of Lodz, which was not occupied by the Soviet army in 1939. His response was curt: "We are not sending Jews to a Polish army."

The visit to the military commissar was even less successful. He threatened me with arrest if I refused to go to work. My intuition told me that I must fight for my life. I would have to escape. Escape! This time it would be very dangerous, since I was now in the Red Army. If something were to go wrong during the escape, the consequences would be dire. But remaining in the coal mine was probably equally dangerous. Decide! Fast!

I decided to escape on the first available train. Without travel documents I would be considered a Red Army deserter. Think fast! Come up with a reasonable plan! The train is leaving soon!

1
Fleeing the Nazis to the "Soviet Paradise"

1
German Occupation and Terror

The news was shocking and devastating. The German *Wehrmacht* staged provocations in several border areas and overran the Polish defenses. Poland was attacked and involved in a war that it had desperately tried to avoid. On September 1, 1939, World War II started.

Despite the news, the weather that Friday morning was nice and the sun was shining like nothing had happened. On that day I found myself at Uncle David's place, on 53 Cegielniana Street, in the city of Lodz, Poland, where I was helping run his grocery store. *Pan* (Mr.) Jozef, the building caretaker, started out the day as usual. He put on his high-heeled boots, attached the hose to the water faucet, and started washing the brick-red interior yard. It was a very solid, beautiful edifice, five stories high. The tenants were mostly upper middle class, businessmen and professionals.

September 1 was usually the day when the new school year started. However, that morning children did not go to school. People were glued to the radio, listening to the news. The first military communiqués did not reveal how bad the situation already was.

By noon the city government of Lodz organized a rally in Plac Wolnosci (Freedom Square), in which I joined together with several hundred thousand people. We listened to the pronouncement by Poland's president Ignacy Moscicki. A few words remain in my memory: "*Oswiadczam wobec Boga i Historii*, I take God and history as my witness" as he described the aggression of Germany against our fatherland. It was a very solemn speech, and it made a strong impression on me. I felt that I was participating in a momentous historic event. Although my spirits and patriotism should have been lifted, I was also aware of the brutality of the Nazi aggressors. I was only fourteen, but I knew that the Nazis mistreated people in occupied Czechoslovakia, in Austria, and in Germany itself. I was frightened and apprehensive about the future.

The war was not unexpected. I had heard Hitler's screaming speeches accompanied by wild cries of "*Sieg Heil!*" Hitler demanded that Poland give up the territories between East Prussia and the rest of Germany, the corridor that also contained the city of Gdansk (Danzig), which, according to the Treaty of Versailles, was a free city, inhabited by Poles and Germans. He called for more *Lebensraum* (living space) for Germans at the expense of other nations. His anti-Semitism was vitriolic, inciting hate and violence.

We didn't have to wait long that day to experience the Luftwaffe's bombs, which fell near the building where I was, by the railway station Lodz Fabryczna, presumably their target. For some reason, most of the residents of 53 Cegielniana Street would assemble by the gate during the bombardments. There they felt safer in the company of other people than staying alone in their apartments or even in the shelters. During one of the bombardments a rumor spread that the Germans were using poison gas. People panicked. Nobody was prepared for such a possibility. Some put wet handkerchiefs over their mouths. After a while we realized that there was no gas.

In the first days of the war we were confident that the Polish Army, with the help of the French and British, would be able to repel the aggressor. France and Great Britain declared war against Germany on September 3. We also believed in Marshal Edward Smigly-Rydz (who had replaced Marshal Jozef Pilsudski after his death in 1935), who had launched in the previous several months a public-relations campaign under the slogan: "Strong, United and Ready." On a large poster he was depicted against skies filled with Polish warplanes. The whole nation was ready to defend its independence, and the Polish Army was putting up a strong resistance, but the *Wehrmacht* overwhelmed it in the first days of the war.

On Wednesday night, September 6, commotion and cries woke me up. We were sleeping in our clothes, as in the previous couple of nights, in case we had to run to shelter. At first, I couldn't understand why everyone was preparing to leave, why the tears and panic. Soon I learned that, according to broadcast announcements, the Germans were rapidly approaching the city and the government was calling on all men capable of bearing arms to immediately leave the city and head toward Warsaw. Hundreds of people, not only men, were leaving town. Uncle David was leaving as well, since he was subject to mobilization at any moment.

Everyone was surprised at the speed with which German troops were advancing toward our city. The common wisdom, derived from experience in World War I, held that it would take the Germans two to three months to reach Lodz, more than 190 miles from the Polish-German border. Instead, they were approaching the city at a rate that would bring them there in five days.

Late that Wednesday night, I left Uncle David's home and hurried to my parents on 8 Wesola Street, a distance of about three miles. In the wee hours of the morning, I arrived home to discover that our room was locked. The landlord gave me the news that everybody had already left. I felt abandoned and couldn't understand why my parents had made such a decision. Father was not at the age likely to be mobilized. My mother and sisters and my baby brother were not ordered to leave the city. What were my parents thinking? Where were they going? And did they believe that they could move faster than the advancing German army? There was no logic in their decision! They must have been caught up in the panic spread not only by the government's call, but also by the neighbors who were fleeing. "Everybody is leaving, we must go," must have been their panicked thought.

I asked the landlord to let me use a ladder to enter our second-floor room through a window to pick up some clothes, which I thought I might need during the coming autumn chill. I stood alone on Wesola Street, seeing no familiar faces, wondering what I should do next, full of fear that something terrible could happen to my family. After all, it was much safer in the city, where one could hide, than to wander under open skies without any protection.

I decided to see whether my oldest sister, Chana, who lived at 15 Stary Rynek, was still at home. When I arrived, her husband had already left, but she was home with her two babies. During the next few dramatic days, I stayed with them.

Thursday, the sixth day of the war, started with intense artillery shelling. It was the first time I experienced a full night of bombardment. We were in the shelter in the basement of the building, and the sound of the shelling was magnified within its walls. Most of the buildings on Stary Rynek had basements that served as warehouses for stores on the first floor. The buildings were old and rather shaky. Children were crying, and the grownups reacted with fear at the building's trembling.

I had seen many retreating Polish soldiers on Thursday but only a few on Friday. They were tired, dirty, and dispirited, many of them wounded though capable of walking. The air was filled with the smell of exploding artillery shells. The city government was not functioning; its staff probably left on Wednesday, along with many others. We learned that an interim committee had formed to replace the city government. It was hastily decided to remove all the patriotic posters, to avoid offending the Germans. People were scrubbing the walls clean.

Friday, at twilight, the first Germans entered the city. I expected that this would be the most dreadful moment of my life. I could not imagine how I would be able to face such an event. Somehow I overcame my fear, eager to witness everything that was happening. I went out in front of the building. The first German soldiers arrived after a couple of hours of ominous silence. They came on motorcycles, a driver and a man in the sidecar, driving fast down Nowomiejska-Zgierska Street, then turning around and coming back. They may have been a forward unit, sent to report whether there was opposition, or, perhaps, I thought, they had missed the city government buildings on Plac Wolnosci about half a mile south of us. So began the German occupation and the frightful life to come.

On Saturday morning large units of the German army entered the city. Soldiers from a cavalry unit came into the yard of 15 Stary Rynek, which had a well, to get water for their horses. This was the time when I could look them right in the eyes and gauge the measure of their hostility. To my surprise, they were rather polite, joking, happy victors. Many of them were blond, and a surprisingly large percentage wore glasses. There was no killing of anybody, yet!

Over the next several days, I could witness the whole might of the German army passing through. Mechanized troops in trucks and artillery pieces with long barrels, which I had never seen before, began a relentless drive forward, day and night, at full speed, rushing to conquer the entire country. I did not see any tank units. Maybe they were roaming through the outskirts of Lodz, avoiding the city streets.

After occupying Lodz the Germans continued their offensive toward Warsaw, the capital. The Polish Army fought gallantly. We heard about the heroic defense of Westerplatte, the fortress protecting Gdansk's harbor. Also mentioned in military bulletins was the fierce battle near Kutno, a town between the western city of Poznan and Warsaw. The ultimate prize for the Germans, of course, was Warsaw, which held out until September 27, under severe daily bombardment by the Luftwaffe.

The final nail in Poland's coffin was the occupation of the eastern part of the country by the Red Army. The partition of Poland was agreed upon in a secret protocol attached to the Molotov-Ribentrop Pact between Germany and the Soviet Union, signed one week before the war started. For Poland it was a treacherous act, rightly called a stab in the back. The Red Army moved into those territories on September 17, after most of the Polish Army was defeated or on the run to the eastern and southern regions of the country.

The German blitzkrieg in Poland succeeded beyond imagination. Poland's air force was largely destroyed on the ground in the first days of the war. Inadequately equipped infantry divisions and cavalry units armed with lances were no match for the German panzer divisions and mobile motorized infantry. Polish bravery alone could not stop the avalanche.

At the end of the first week of occupation, I went back home to find that my parents and siblings, except for my brother Sam, had returned, all unharmed. They were the lucky ones. The Luftwaffe attacked thousands of people heading toward Warsaw. Unarmed civilians vainly tried to find cover from the bombers flying low over the potato fields, and were systematically shot. It was a massacre. Did I say that they hadn't killed anybody yet? Clearly, I was wrong!

My older brother Samuel, who walked faster than anyone else in our family, managed to reach Warsaw to find out that there was no mobilization. There he endured the cruel bombardment of the city over the next three weeks, running from one burning building to another. After several more weeks, he too returned home, but in very bad shape, limping from injuries and exhausted. He remained in bed for several weeks to regain his health and strength. But he was young, and he made it. His safe return was to play a critical role in my life.

The terror against the civilian population started almost immediately. Germans ordered all Jews to wear a yellow Star of David on their clothing, allowing them to distinguish between Jews and others. At the same time, Jews were forbidden to use the city streetcar that went to the downtown area (beyond Plac Wolnosci to Piotrkowska, the main street). Whenever the Germans needed people for work, to unload coal, to repair something, to move their people into abandoned or emptied houses, they rounded up Jews off the street. Several military trucks would suddenly stop; soldiers would hurry out, calling, "*Kome, kome*," and would chase people trying to run away. As a rule, the Germans did not feed the detained, prodding them to work harder, constantly yelling, "*Schnell, schnell,*" and frequently beating them. Most of the time, they let the exhausted people go when the work was done. My brother Samuel and I were caught several times for such work. Simultaneously German soldiers started the public humiliation of shaving the beards of Ortho- dox Jews in front of smiling onlookers. Many times they shaved not only the beard but also the skin, causing the victims to bleed profusely. I saw such pictures printed in Polish newspapers, which by then had come under Ger- man management, of soldiers enjoying tormenting the *Verfluchte Juden*— damned Jews.

For a while, though, life returned to some semblance of normality. My uncle's grocery store reopened and, from time to time, German officers visited it. They were surprised to see that soap had not disappeared from the shelves. Apparently, there was a shortage of soap in Germany. In our area, around Wesola Street, it was very difficult to get bread and other food items. We had to be on the street long before curfew ended at 6 A.M. to be in the queue before the bakery opened. We managed to avoid German patrols by hiding behind the gates of houses surrounding the bakery.

Sometime in late September or early October 1939, rumors spread that, ac- cording to the agreement between the Soviets and Germans, Lodz would be turned over to the Soviets. The rationale was that the old border between the Germans and the Russians that existed before World War I would be restored, and at that time the Russians had occupied Lodz. The rumors were reinforced by the sight of a Soviet flag on the *Województwo* (provincial administrative office) on Zachodnia Street. This building had been the beautiful mansion owned by the Jewish textile magnate Israel Poznanski. Many people, includ- ing myself, walked to the place to verify that alongside the German flag a red Soviet flag was now displayed on the balcony. It was believed to demonstrate that a Soviet delegation was visiting the city and negotiating the transfer of Lodz. In light of the terror applied by the Nazis, it was hoped that the Soviets would introduce a much more lenient occupation regime.

Unfortunately, the Soviet flag was only an illusion created by the wind. What had actually happened was that a red Nazi flag had been twisted by the wind so that the swastika was hidden from view.

Among the first prominent subjects of German terror were synagogues. Fire and dynamite destroyed them. I was deeply attached to the large and beautiful Wolborska Street synagogue. That's where I attended services and listened to the wonderful choir, led by Professor Yitzhak Zaks. Many of my classmates from the Jakuba 10 Talmud Torah School sang in that choir, to which I also aspired to be admitted. Other synagogues, on Zachodnia 56 and on Aleje Kosciuszko 2, were also destroyed by the German occupiers.

Terror in the city intensified. There were shootings for any minor insubordination or for no reason. An ominous sign of what we could expect in the future was the Germans' attempt to destroy the tall monument of Tadeusz Kosciuszko on Plac Wolnosci. Kosciuszko was our most revered national hero, the symbol of Poland's struggle for independence. A group of Jews was compelled to destroy the granite monument; whether the Jews didn't try hard enough or their tools were inadequate, not much damage was done to the monument after several days' work. However, it did much damage to the Jews. This arrangement by the Nazis, in which Jews were set to bring down the symbol of Polish national heroism and freedom, was a clear subterfuge to provoke anti-Jewish sentiment among Poles. As November 11 approached, the anniversary of the 1918 armistice and German defeat and also Poland's Independence Day, the occupiers desired to commemorate it with the fall of Kosciuszko's monument.

On the night of November 11, a loud explosion was heard. The next morning, when I went to Plac Wolnosci, the Kosciuszko monument was lying in ruin. I wasn't aware then of the attempt to blame the Jews for the destruction of the monument, thereby inciting the Polish population and creating an excuse for punishing the Jews by destroying their shrines. Nevertheless, the Nazis destroyed all the synagogues in Lodz.

From the very beginning of the German occupation Christian Poles were terrorized as well. In most cities the first victims were intellectuals, prominent leaders, members of political parties. Poles were to be considered an inferior race, destined to serve the German *Herrenvolk* (masters). The destruction of the Kosciuszko monument was a powerful sign of the occupier's attitude toward the Polish nation. A tragic phase of our history had just begun. Our hope that Great Britain and France would fulfill their commitment to come to our defense against the German aggression vanished. The two most powerful countries in Europe were not willing or able to keep their promises. In the summer of 1940 France could not even defend itself against the onslaught of overwhelming Nazi forces. Poland had to face its destiny alone.

SWEDEN

Baltic Sea

Gulf of Riga

ESTONIA

LATVIA

LITHUANIA

EAST PRUSSIA

● Gdansk

● Wilno

GERMANY

● Poznan

✪ Warszawa

● Bialystok

U.S.S.R.

● Lodz

● Lublin

● Kielce

● Luck

● Krakow
Auschwitz

● Lwow

CHECHOSLOVAKIA

HUNGARY

ROMANIA

N

0   50   100 kilometers
0   50   100 miles

☐ Territories Occupied by Germany
▨ Territories Occupied by U.S.S.R.

1. Partition of Poland, September 1939

2
Escape from Occupied Poland

The city was buzzing with rumors, as many planned to get out from under German occupation. The only realistic place to go was the Polish territories occupied by the Soviet Union. The new frontier was temporarily open for crossing in both directions. When this subject came up in our family conversations, my father's reaction was negative. His point was that neither Hitler nor Stalin was allowing Jews to practice their religion; hence, we might as well stay where we were. How wrong was my dear father! Yes, one could not freely pray under either regime, but the chance of saving one's life was much greater under Stalin. This became clear later; at the end of 1939, nobody could foresee that, under Hitler, the possibility of surviving would be extremely slim.

Among the destinations in Soviet-occupied Poland were the cities of Bialystok and Lwow. To reach them, refugees took the trains that were running well on the German side and infrequently and overloaded on the Soviet side. Apparently even Germans provided transport to the frontier for good money. Once a military truck parked and stayed for two days on Wesola Street, where we lived—was it transporting escapees to the new German-Soviet border? People suspected that, but I never learned whether this was actually the case.

My older brother Sam and I got together with three young men and Mr. Zylberszatz, all neighbors from our building, to discuss the possibility of escape. Only Zylberszatz was married, and he had two daughters. He intended to go to the Soviet occupied territories, find a place to live, and return for his family. His plan seemed rational, but he was counting on free movement across the new frontier continuing. Unfortunately, events were to show that such hope was naïve.

My plans to leave with the others were initially met with concern by my parents. Mother said often that I was too young to cope with the difficulties of flight; that Father didn't intend to go; nor did my sisters or, of course, my brother Yitzhak, who was only nine. What a contrast to my parents' hasty decision to leave the city in the first days of the war! It is quite possible that the experience of that journey influenced their decision. They had seen what it meant to be exposed to the German military in the open and how difficult it was to survive without food and shelter. By comparison, staying at home, even under the harsh situation known to them at the time, seemed a better alternative.

Leaving my parents and siblings was a very difficult and painful decision. It was not a youthful dream of a fantastic adventure; I was not an adventurous teenager craving travel to faraway countries. My upbringing was shaped by the limited opportunities offered by the milieu of our poor neighborhood. Even though I attended Zionist meetings with my sister Esther, I had not aspired to go to Palestine as many young people did.

I heard enough warnings from Mother about the difficulties and understood the dangers that lay ahead. Despite these warnings, the fear of remaining under German occupation drove me to my decision. Intuitively, I felt that the future under the Nazis would be very bleak. I couldn't then imagine complete annihilation of the Jewish people, but I realized that the Nazis were capable of killing at a whim, based on what I had seen of their behavior in the few months of the occupation. And I had read about their atrocities in occupied Czechoslovakia and Austria.

In addition, I had an exaggerated notion of how good it would be in the Soviet Union. That idea was not based on any ideological sympathy to Communism, about which I knew almost nothing. I knew very little about the Soviet regime. In my analysis, escaping to the Soviet Union was the only possibility. I was not mature enough to convey my fears to the others in my family and convince them that we all should leave Poland. I feel selfish and to this day cannot forgive myself for my inability to bring them with me.

I told my older brother Sam that I intended to escape with him and the others from our building on Wesola #8. I never received any clear acceptance; nor did they try to dissuade me from going with them. The group let me be present during the plans for escape without concern that I might carelessly reveal their intentions. They understood better than I did that we would have little chance to remain together all the way to the Soviet side. Sooner or later, they probably thought, in the unavoidable turmoil everybody would have to face each new situation on his own. Nevertheless, we intended to attempt to escape as a group.

My preparations for that journey consisted of getting a few shirts, my new woolen sweater, and some money. I continued working in my uncle's store, and he gave me extra money, in addition to the usual tips I was still able to collect from delivering groceries to customers. My uncle was sympathetic to my plan, but Aunt Sara chided me for my intention to go to the "Reds." She knew more about the Reds than I did, but was wrong nevertheless.

I didn't know the exact day my brother and the others had decided to go, although I felt that it was imminent and I was prepared. I learned from our cousin Anna Szrojt that it was possible to survive many days on sugar and cocoa. I made sure that I had a sufficient supply of those things in my knapsack, but had still to get a loaf of bread. While I was waiting in a queue to buy bread my younger sister Shajndl rushed in to tell me to hurry home because the group was leaving. She saved my life. It was the last time I saw Shajndl.

I wish I could recall other episodes of my last day with my parents and family. I must have said goodbye to all of them. Was I crying? I don't think so. I was probably fully concentrating on the escape and the difficulties that lay ahead and on trying to leave home showing how brave I was. I may also have inherited from my father the trait of keeping my feelings inside. I was sure that by not dramatizing I would not cause unnecessary pain to them. I did not tell Yitzhak, whom I loved so deeply, that I was leaving, maybe forever, because I did not want him to cry. He was always a joyous child. I do not remember where Esther was. She played such an important role in my life and intellectual development. The most I can recall about the last minutes is a picture I hold in my memory: I am putting on the knapsack, looking around the room and saying farewell to everybody.

3
"So You Want to Go to the Soviet Paradise?"

Our journey started on a rainy day—appropriate weather for the occasion. We ordered a horse cab. Mother and my older sister Dvojra (Dora) saw us off, hidden in a gate on nearby Bazarna Street. It is difficult to describe the scene I remember so clearly. No doubt they were sad. But I also had the feeling that they were proud of us, hoping that our journey would be successful and that we might even be able to help them as well. This is not what they told us, but what I think I read in their sad and anxious faces.

It was late November 1939. On the way to the Lodz Fabryczna train station, no German soldier stopped us. Even though there were many Jews in the station, everything went smoothly, without incident. I think the Germans were not interested in preventing us from leaving their area of occupation. However, the SS clearly desired to provide us with a farewell beating, and they found a convenient place for it. After a short journey to Koluszki, we had to change trains going to Warsaw. There we had to move through a small underground passage and go up to another track. A huge crowd was going downstairs to reach the passage. At that point, SS officers were indiscriminately beating the crowd over the head with truncheons. Luckily, they couldn't hit everyone and they missed the shorter people, of which I was one. This was the first time I had been in the middle of a beating. I remember it so well that after more than sixty years I can still paint an exact picture of it. Each time I see movie beatings with truncheons, it reminds me of that experience. It was a clear confirmation that my decision to flee was amply justified. Somehow, Sam also passed through the dangerous spot and avoided the SS farewell beating. But we lost contact with the others in our group, never seeing them again. We continued our journey to Warsaw without additional incidents.

An unexpected evening arrival in Warsaw made our situation more precarious. When we left the train station the curfew was already in force. Walking along the deserted main street we were afraid of being stopped by the Germans. They were not reticent about shooting anyone who appeared on the street after the curfew. Suddenly, some people peering out from the gate of a building on Aleje Jerozolimskie called to us. They asked if we were fleeing the Germans and needed a place to stay overnight. These generous people, religious Jews, had a very nice apartment and several more guests like us. Our hosts treated us to some food, and we didn't mind sleeping on the floor. All this was done free of any charge, just to help people fleeing the Nazis.

The next day, we took a horse cart across the magnificent Poniatowski Bridge to the train station in Praga, across the Vistula River on the east side of Warsaw, where trains departed for the east. There were many Jews on that train and a sizable number of Christians. Malkinia was the last station on the German side of the new frontier with the Soviet Union. There, German soldiers ordered the Jews to one side and Christian Poles to the other.

The Jewish group, which numbered close to a thousand, was shown the road to take. Along that country road German soldiers set up several checkpoints in front of which escapees formed long lines. Aware of the difficulties awaiting them on the journey, most people had little knapsacks, with money and provisions. The soldiers who did the checking were polite. They just took money, watches, and other valuables, often with a smile. After being checked, people would put their remaining belongings back in the sacks as quickly as possible and continue along the road to the next checkpoint.

It's amazing how inventive and ingenious one can become when faced with danger. The procedure gave me and my brother Sam an idea: while still some distance from the head of the line, we would mix up all the things inside our knapsack, then walk down the road, pretending that we had already been checked. Luckily it worked; as the soldiers were concentrating on grabbing valuables from their current victim, they weren't watching what else went on.

Having passed those dangerous spots, we were confronted with the Gestapo. Again we learned the kind of butchers they were. About two hundred yards past the final checkpoint stood a small building, perhaps a little village school. In front of the building SS or Gestapo officers were watching each passerby, occasionally calling someone inside the house. There they beat the chosen victim nearly to death, leaving them with broken bones and bloodied heads. We were to see hundreds of such poor souls over the next several days. But we were lucky again.

The last German soldier I met at the 1939 Soviet-German border before entering the so-called neutral zone was very polite and even kind. He didn't ask for our knapsacks; he didn't beat us. He only asked the ironic question: "So you are going to the Soviet paradise?" and offered me a cigarette. Just a few minutes before the Germans were robbing and beating Jews for the sheer pleasure of it. Then this one soldier made us believe that there were still some decent human beings left in the nation that so abruptly and overwhelmingly turned into murderers.

Maybe I was under the influence of propaganda, about the paradise in the Soviet Union. I recall when I was about eight years old, while walking with my friend Zelig, we stopped in front of a grocery store. We saw some candies in the window and Zelig said, "You know what? In Russia, children can have candy free." I don't know where he got this idea, but it stuck in my mind and perhaps was a factor in my favorable impression of the country I was about to enter. The reality, however, was quite different. Instead of a welcome to the paradise, soldiers' bayonets and a closed border met us.

When we arrived, the border had already been closed for several days. About ten thousand refugees, including many elderly people, children, and those injured by Gestapo torture, were camping in despair under the open sky without food, water, or knowledge when and how this ordeal would end. In the next several days many more thousands arrived, but the border remained closed. We were trapped between the Germans' desire to get rid of us, and the Soviets, to whom we were unwelcome guests.

After several days the situation became unbearable. The only water source was located in the neutral zone, closer to the German than to the Soviet side. People tried desperately to get some water, but the Germans would shoot at them. The only hope was the Soviets. But their orders were firm: "Don't let them in!"

From time to time, desperate people tried to run past the Soviet soldiers. Each time the border guards would shoot at them, aiming at their legs. Although this could have stopped a few, it would not work for all the thousands camping there. Therefore, as we became more desperate we began to storm the border by force of numbers, pushing ourselves past the bayonets of the

Soviet guards. At first, we were gentle; we just pushed ahead and the Soviets pushed us back, yelling, "*Davay nazad* (go back)." Men would open their shirts, baring their chests, calling to the soldiers, "Shoot!" They would not. The next attempt to break through was better organized. Women with children, as well as those who had been tortured by the Gestapo, went in front. Then, strong young men pushed ahead. We were thousands and they were only a few platoons on the frontier. We overwhelmed them, pushed them aside, and crossed the border. Feeling victorious, the huge column of refugees started singing proletarian songs and marched ahead. Then reinforcements arrived on horses and pushed us back. No victory yet! It was already the seventh or eighth day since we arrived at the border. Sam and I had swollen legs and hands caused by cold and hunger. Many times I recalled Mother warning me that it will be very difficult. A few more days and it could end in a catastrophe. Medical assistance was not available, the food ran out, and it started snowing. I wandered around that huge place without hope, where whole families with elderly members and small children were camping on the frozen soil, with hardly any blankets.

Through all of this, though, there were some comic moments as well. In the middle of the open space between the borders stood one large barn, full of straw. This was the only place where one could warm up and even get a little sleep under a roof. There were hundreds upon hundreds of people inside the barn. New arrivals at night had to walk through the darkness, stepping over lying bodies until some little space could be found up high. Those left outside, and there were thousands of them, wanted to go in for a while, but could do it only if the insiders could somehow be lured out. And the "outsiders" found a workable trick: yelling that the Soviets had opened the borders for one hour only. Obviously nobody wanted to miss this opportunity. People left the barn in a hurry. Then the outsiders went in. After several such tricks, everybody knew it wasn't true. Yet despite that awareness, people would still leave the barn, thinking, "this time, maybe it's true."

The next day more refugees arrived and the crowd got bigger and even more determined to break through. The next storm against the Soviet border was very strong. After several hours of pushing, yelling, and screaming, we broke through. This time we went far inside Soviet territory, perhaps a mile or so. We triumphantly marched along the road and people intoned proletarian songs. Again a strong cavalry unit met us and managed to push us back, but we gained experience and learned how to scatter along the road. When we broke through the next time, the troops were unable to push us back. Yet although we penetrated more deeply, it by no means meant that we were free to continue on.

The commander of the cavalry unit who met us about three miles inside Soviet territory started negotiating with us. He asked why we were coming over to their side. People in front told him that we were fleeing the fascists and we wanted to lead a productive life in the Soviet Union.

"Are you working-class people?" the commander asked.

"Sure we are. Look at our hands!"

"If you promise not to push any further, I will ask at headquarters if we can let you in."

"Yes, we promise."

"Then," said the commander, "wait here. It will take me two to three hours to return." We promised to behave and waited anxiously for his return. Then afar we saw him riding back bringing the good news that we were allowed to enter the USSR. Hurray!

The reason why the border was closed was never explained. Was there a date when the movement across the new frontier was supposed to stop? Or was the rumor true that a group of refugees tried to rob a bank in Minsk and we were punished for this?

There are at least two broader questions: why were the millions of Jews living in Poland not coming to the same conclusion as a few hundred thousand did, to flee the Nazis for the Soviet side? Unfortunately, most Jews based their thinking on the relatively moderate treatment of eastern European Jews by the Germans during World War I. The second question is, if a million or so refugees had come, would the Soviets have let them in? I think the Soviets could have found a place for them in their vast country. In 1940 they transferred several hundred thousand people to Siberia and other outlying regions. They could have done the same to a much larger number of refugees. Although they were put to work in severe weather and under very harsh physical conditions I have no doubt that the percentage of survivors would have been far greater than was the case under the Nazis.

4
From Bialystok to Novosibirsk

Immediately after we got permission to enter the Soviet-occupied territories, soldiers began to register us. To the question where we wanted to go, nearly everyone said Moscow or Leningrad. They dutifully wrote this down without a smile. We didn't understand how naïve our wishes were. Very few Soviet citizens were allowed to settle in those large metropolitan centers because of overcrowding.

I registered my birthday as May 1, 1923, instead of 1925 in order to be eligible to work (the working age was sixteen in the USSR). After these formalities, we were free to continue our journey. I don't recall the Soviets providing us with any food. We undertook a march of four or five miles to the nearest village, Zaremby Koscielne, where we arrived late in the evening. For the first time in nine days we slept in a warm place and got hot food. We paid with money and with a few pairs of socks.

The next day we learned that the trains were running only sporadically from the village and that we would have a better chance to catch a train in the city of Lapy, twenty miles further. Without hesitation, we undertook the march to Lapy. Our goal was Bialystok, a large city with a sizable Jewish population. At Lapy, trains ran infrequently and were always extremely crowded. People even climbed on the roofs of the cars just to get a chance to reach Bialystok. On our second or third attempt, we got on a train and arrived safely.

The city looked neat and clean, without any war damage. By the time we arrived, tens of thousands of refugees were in the city of about 100,000 prewar residents, about half of them Jews.

The obvious place to go in a strange city was the synagogue. It was overwhelmed with refugees. We found a spot on the floor and spent several nights there. Jews from Bialystok were very friendly to the refugees. We were invited to a Jewish home for a Sabbath meal of the traditional *chulent* (potatoes, meat, barley, and beans baked overnight in the bakery's oven and retrieved Saturday at noontime after the prayers). The city's calm and friendly attitude toward the newcomers was partly the result of having so far escaped the trauma of war.

After a few days in Bialystok, Jewish leaders offered a large group of refugees, including us, shelter in a resort area seven miles outside the city, where city residents used to spend their summer vacations. It was a large village with rather primitive housing, without water, sewage, or heating, and the windows were broken in most of the bungalows. Nevertheless, it was much less crowded than the synagogues, a regular food supply was organized, and life took on some semblance of normalcy.

It was now December with freezing nights. We had been assigned to a house with some families with small children. Therefore, we had priority for a little oven built of bricks in the middle of the room. The windows were not repaired, and sleeping on the floor was very cold. My sweater served me well at night, helping to keep my legs warm, and my light coat became my blanket. This was certainly better than the conditions along the Soviet-German border. When the windows were fixed, we could have stayed comfortably there, but the Soviet authorities had different plans for us.

The Soviets were recruiting refugees for work deep in the USSR. They offered a year's contract for work in a particular city, and after its expiration we would be free to go anyplace in the USSR. The offices formalizing these contracts were located in Bialystok. During the severe winter of 1940, with temperatures reaching −30°F, we had to walk about fifteen miles to reach the city and then return. My clothes were not adequate for this weather. In Poland boys my age did not yet wear long pants, even in winter. The typical outfit was short pants and socks and relatively light shoes (leather or made of resin). In addition, my parents couldn't afford to buy me a good winter coat that would have compensated for my lightweight clothing.

If I was ever a burden to my older brother Sam, this was one of those times. We started our journey on a very frosty morning, and after several miles, I began to feel acutely frostbitten. In a house on the way we warmed up and got a glass of hot milk. It helped initially, and we continued on our way, but the chill got to me again very soon. Ever more frequently I begged my brother to let us stop and warm up in a house. I could no longer endure the cold. Parts of my body started freezing. I cried. I felt unable to go on.

Somehow, with many stops on the way, we reached the city. We registered for work in the city of Omsk, in the western part of Siberia. We got new Soviet temporary documents and an advance of more than a hundred rubles. We felt good and set out to return to our village to prepare for our departure a few days later.

We had not gone far when we realized that someone had stolen my brother's Soviet travel document. Without it, we couldn't leave. We returned to the office where we had received our assignment and reported the lost document to the military officer. He began to shout: "You swindlers, you parasites, what did you do with the money?" It took us several attempts to get through to him that we didn't lose the money, only the document. Finally it sunk in that we might not be swindlers after all, since we didn't claim to have lost the money. He calmed down, took my document and assignment, and started preparing new ones. This time it was for Novosibirsk, deeper into Siberia.

A few days later we reported to the assembly point and departed. On the way to Novosibirsk, we learned a famous Russian song, "*Katiusha*" (this diminutive of the name Catherine was adopted for the most powerful Soviet piece of artillery in the war). We fell in love with this serene, peaceful song and sang it many times during the journey. The lyrics paint a picture of blooming apple and pear trees, and a mist-draped bank on the river where Katiusha sings of her love for her boyfriend who is away defending their country, and she promises to be faithful. The song was a necessary antidote to the miserable conditions we traveled in.

Our train consisted of many freight cars, or as we called them, cattle trucks. On each side of the car there were two levels of bunks and an iron stove in the middle, which was always red hot. It was a very severe winter that year, and we were moving across Russia toward the Ural Mountains and Siberia, where winter is always unbearable for those not accustomed to it. The walls inside the car were white with frost, especially in the corners and near the doors, where cold air penetrated. The red-hot stove could not warm up the inside of the car, except in its closest proximity. There were no toilets in the cars, and no water.

The journey lasted twenty-one days, as we had the lowest priority in the overburdened Soviet railroad system. This was during the Soviet Union's war with Finland, which strained the railway system to the utmost. Nevertheless, the authorities treated us fairly whenever possible. At railway stations in larger cities we were served dinner in the station restaurants, closed to the public during the time we were there. Despite those good intentions, on many occasions we didn't arrive at the time when the dinner was ready. A few times we had dinner late, even after midnight. But we were grateful, since we had only "dry rations" between those meals. *Kipiatok,* meaning boiled hot water, was one of the first Russian words we learned. *Kipiatok* signs, posted in each large or small railway station, mark one of the best inventions of the Russian railroad system. A cup of hot tea and a piece of bread were often our meal during those cold days and nights. For our physical needs we could use the frequent short stops in areas far from any buildings.

Our train was usually parked on secondary lines, sometimes far away from the railway station, where we would go for the prepared dinners or to buy something to eat in addition to the rations. On my walk from the car to the station in Chelabinsk, I got serious frostbite in my foot. Although we were not far from the main building, at temperatures of −40°F it was easy to get frostbite wearing only light leather shoes and thin socks. My foot took months to heal.

While in the large railway stations we could meet local people. Some of them looked poor and we did not have a chance to talk to them, since we did not know the Russian language well enough, but also because of their unwillingness to engage in conversation with strangers. I regretted that our ability to observe the places we passed through was extremely limited by the absence of windows. The only chance to look around was on our way to the railway stations for meals. The stations never looked attractive anyway. But then we approached the snowy, tall Ural Mountains, a majestic view entirely new to me. This was the biggest thrill of that long journey.

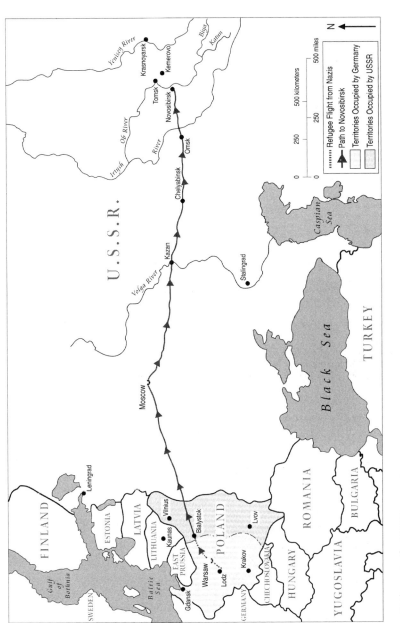

2. Refugee in the USSR, 1939–41

5
A Lavish Reception for the Liberated Belorussians

We arrived in Novosibirsk late in the afternoon of a sunny day in the beginning of February 1940 and were immediately transferred from the railroad to a public bath by very strange-looking buses of a kind we had never seen before, bulky (resembling today's American school buses), painted a light yellow color, and with the windows painted by the Siberian frost.

Everyone received new violet-colored underwear, warm quilted cotton pants, a *kufajka* (short cotton-stuffed overcoat), and a pair of *valonki* (woolen footwear). This was a proper outfit for the Siberian winter. After the wonderful bath and new clothes, more pleasant surprises were awaiting us. Back on the same buses, we traveled to our dormitory, a large, unfinished six-story building. The authorities hastily finished three floors for the newcomers and placed families with children on the third floor and single people on the fourth and fifth. We were assigned to a large room for six single men. The iron beds were covered with new blankets and white bed linen. Next to each bed was placed a small *tumbetchka* (bedside table) and a chair. A tin kettle with *kipiatok* was on a table in the middle of the room. There were no decorations on the walls except a black disk, eight inches in diameter, which served as a radio receiver. It transmitted the official program and we could only regulate the volume. Every once in a while, a woman would knock at the door bringing fresh hot water for tea. There was also a large oven in a kitchen on the third floor where all the residents could cook their meals.

It was about 8:00 or 9:00 P.M. when we finally settled in our room. Then we were invited for a reception. The food included a varied assortment of fish, some (for example, sturgeon) we had never seen before. There was a selection of cold meat cuts, breads, fruits, and cookies. It was instant "Communism" since we could eat as much as we desired, and at the end some food was still left over. A professional dance ensemble performed Russian folk dances for us. We were immensely impressed by the performance.

Early in the morning after a short night's sleep, visitors knocked at our door. Senior party and government officials of Novosibirsk had come to welcome us while we were still in bed. Richly dressed and looking content and healthy, they greeted us: "Good morning, comrades. Welcome to our city. We are glad to have you here, brothers from Belorussia. How was your terrible life under the *Polskye pany* (Polish masters)?"

Instead of being treated as political refugees, the Soviet authorities designated us as "liberated Belorussians." Initially we were privileged guests and were offered a Soviet passport. Even though accepting Soviet citizenship could have prevented future return to Poland, our deep desire to be recognized as equal among others prevailed. We considered this as an opportunity to cease to be a persecuted minority.

It was a surprising part of our welcome. How highly they regarded us, how caring and happy they were that we finally had been liberated from Polish oppression. We didn't understand the attention; they must have been directed to put on an impressive show of the Soviet system, and they really prepared one for us. Since Bialystok had been incorporated by the Soviet authorities into the Belorussian Soviet Republic, we who arrived from that city were called "Liberated Belorussians." This identification as Belorussian had far-reaching consequences for us, which we had no way of foreseeing.

While all this took place, on the first floor hundreds of people were forming an early morning queue to buy a loaf of bread at a grocery store, which was to open at 7:00 A.M. The first floor was still an unfinished construction site, filled with the smell of acetylene used in welding. Hundreds of locals were struggling to preserve their place in the queue, contending with others who hoped to cheat their way ahead or who pressed against the entrance of the store when it opened. Even more disturbing was the rule established for entry into the grocery, which permitted the Belorussians to enter without standing in line. The rationale, probably, was that we had come from a terrible country where Polish masters exploited us and had experienced a miserable life thus far and so deserved better treatment in the land of the proletariat.

We got a special corner in the shop where a huge block of butter was put on the counter, along with a selection of sausages and even chocolate. All of these items were not available to local people, in either this or any other store.

What were those people thinking when they saw us buying delicacies not available to them? What a terrible disregard for their own people! At least the authorities should have set up such a special shop in some inconspicuous place. Either they didn't understand or they didn't care what people would think. How terrorized the population must have been to remain silent about the privileges lavished on the Belorussians. They didn't show resentment toward us, but perhaps were able to hide their feelings well. After a few days, when we ventured out to the downtown shops, we learned that the same rule of letting us in without standing in line was in force there as well. Moreover, this was not a short-term arrangement. It lasted the whole first year we were there.

On one of the floors in our living quarters, a *krasnyj ugolok* (red corner) was organized. It was a special room where we could read newspapers and other propaganda material, as well as assemble for lectures. The first night's party was held there. What struck me among the propaganda materials was a story I already knew from reading the German-run paper in Lodz. The subject was Marshal Voroshilov and his marksmen, the *Voroshilovskyi Strielok*. The German occupation paper *Lodzianka* ran a big story about the Red Army, its training and armaments. Among the Goebbels propaganda material was a story about the excellence of the sharpshooters who were trained in a special youth organization, *Osoviachim*. After demonstrating sufficient marksmanship, participants received a badge called *Voroshilovskyi Strielok*. This favorable story seemed incredible in a German paper just a few months after all the Nazi propaganda had been directed against Jews and Bolsheviks. But since September 1939, the Germans and Soviets had become "good friends." Now I saw the propaganda about the grandness of Voroshilov and his sharpshooters at its source, praising him in the same form as in the Goebbels propaganda.

I was not at that time aware that a similar propaganda change took place in the Soviet Union as well. Only recently did I come across an excerpt from foreign minister Molotov's address to the Supreme Soviet in the fall of 1939, where he lashed out at Great Britain and France for their continuation of the war with Germany instead of reaching a peace agreement, accompanied with accusations of imperialistic plans to retain and exploit their colonies.

What a shock! Nazi Germany and Communist Russia on the same propaganda wavelength as if they had never been the most bitter enemies. I could not comprehend what was happening in the world, what it all meant for me and for my family left under Nazi occupation. I was in the middle of a big international game, an observer and possibly a victim as well. My young mind was unable to look ahead and deduce what it might bring in the future. I could not in my wildest imagination think that these two "friends" would in less than two years engage in a titanic battle for survival. I was comfortable and happy to be on this part of the world's stage, facing a completely new and unknown world.

A Soviet officer assembled all Belorussians in the *krasnyj ugolok* and distributed an advance payment for work we had not yet performed. Moreover, we weren't even rushed to accept the jobs that were waiting for us and for which we had come in the first place. Only after several days did they finally start talking about job assignments. Very few people were assigned according to their wishes, experience, or occupational training. Most were sent to the nearby construction site of a textile mill. Even women, who had never worked outside the home at all, not to speak of construction work, were sent there. My brother Sam was assigned to the yard of a nearby sawmill where timber was unloaded. The team he worked with loaded the timber to be sawed and then removed the boards. The temperature during that winter reached nearly forty below, which, when accompanied by strong winds, was extremely dangerous and unbearable. Yet, people were working outside that sawmill and my brother, completely unaccustomed to it, was with them.

Since officially I was only sixteen years old my assignment was to the carpentry shop, located not far from the sawmill. Both these units were parts of the same organization. Within the carpentry section, which produced doors and windows for industrial and residential buildings being erected nearby, was a carpentry school for youngsters my age. The only instructor for the whole group of about thirty boys was Innokenty Grigorevich. He was a military veteran who almost always wore a Red Army hat with earflaps that could be lowered in cold weather, a style that we saw for the first time at the Soviet border when we crossed in 1939. He was a very good storyteller and frequently under the influence of alcohol.

The first day in that shop was very exciting for me and I suppose also for the Russian youngsters. Although I had a few jobs in various places in Lodz, this one was quite different, beginning with the new language. A friendly group introduced themselves to me: Mishas, Fiedias, Grishas, Ivans, and even an Arkashka. The section where the school was located was spacious enough for each trainee to have a work place. I liked the smell coming from the wood scraps and shavings lying all over the place.

The first lesson was about the names of the tools. There was a *rubanok,* a *molotok,* and a *stamiestka* (a plane, hammer, and chisel). I learned fast, and my Russian language capability improved rapidly. More advanced trainees did all the teaching at first. The instructor gave me an introductory lesson on how to operate the plane and showed me what kind of work I had to do. The Russian youngsters were already at work on producing frames for bricks; I never saw the instructor teaching them to make any other product.

At 1:00 P.M. we ran to the *stolovaya* (cafeteria), nearly a mile from the carpentry shop. In the winter we had to be careful not to get frostbite. We would watch each other pointing out little white spots on the cheek that were a sign that the face had started freezing; the remedy was to rub the area immediately with snow. Summer reached the other extreme, of 100°F by midday, although cold in the morning—a characteristic typical of a continental climate. The quilted *kufajka* had to be carried practically all year round.

The cafeteria's most common food was cabbage soup and porridge gruel with a teaspoon of oil on top. The gruel was sometimes grits or cream of wheat. For variety, mashed potatoes would be offered. The menu did not deviate much from the Russian saying: "*Shci y kasha pishcia nasha* (cabbage soup and gruel is our food)."

With the passage of time, we liberated Belorussians started looking around, getting acquainted with local people and learning more about life in Novosibirsk. One of my acquaintances, Sergey, was a very interesting man who lived in the same building. I was not sure what he did for a living. He and his wife were professionals, but their life was odd. They rarely were together; at least at the times I was invited to their apartment. Sergey's hobby was the accordion, which he played very well. I always enjoyed listening to his music, mostly Russian folk melodies, so beautiful and different from melodies we were used to in Poland. He even tried to teach me to play the accordion, but I wasn't good at it.

Sergey and his wife were always friendly and pleasant to me, often offering snacks and seeming to enjoy my company. In his free time Sergey was also the projectionist and mechanic at the movie theater. I used to go there with him, as he showed movies every Saturday and Sunday. He taught me how to operate the film equipment, how to rewind the reel, and how to fix minor problems such as ruptured reels. It seemed to me that his friendly manner may have some hidden aim or was on the order of somebody else. But I never experienced any improper behavior or trouble from him. It is possible that my suspicions were entirely unfair.

Some of the other people's acquaintances enlightened them about real life. One of our friends learned a lot about the recent Stalinist persecutions. He would tell horror stories about people being jailed for nothing or for the smallest transgression. Ten-year sentences were the mild ones. He became obsessed by the subject, overcome by fear that it could happen to any one of us. I didn't understand how real the danger was, and I ignored it.

More immediate and acute were the working conditions for some of the refugees, especially women. Work on a construction site was very hard, since it required heavy lifting, very difficult for a young girl not used to it. Performing those operations under the severe cold of the Siberian winter reaching −40° F was beyond the endurance of women from Poland. In the spring, snow melted into huge puddles and mud covered the streets, making them almost impassable. The poor women would return home exhausted, mud covering their heavy shoes. A few of those young women attempted suicide as a result of nearly unbearable working conditions.

My earnings were very low, 115 rubles, since I was a trainee. My brother's pay was not very high either—about 200–250 rubles. His earnings depended on the amounts the foreman would write down to his credit and the pay per unit. We could afford to have a meal in a restaurant once a month or to buy something in the *kolkhoz* (collective farm) market. Members of the *kolkhoz* sold products to get cash for materials that had to be paid for in rubles. They were paid in products produced during the year. Often such payments were meager because the *kolkhoz* had to deliver a percentage of the crops to the government, to pay for the work and services done by government agricultural machinery and operators. Quite often almost nothing was left for the members. On occasion, collective farmers were allowed to have a goat, cow, or pig for their own; hence on the *kolkhoz* market one could buy milk or a piece of pork or beef. On my first visit to the market in Novosibirsk I saw farmers taking some frozen white pieces of different sizes and shapes from a sack. I was told that this was milk. During much of the winter milk could not be delivered to the market in any container except in a sack, so that it could easily be taken out and cut with an ax.

The earnings of people who managed to get a job in garment factories were somewhat better because they could fill up to 300 percent of the required norm. But then their coworkers resented them for showing that a much higher productivity could be achieved. Local people knew better. Whenever higher productivity was achieved, the pay per unit was lowered (or the norm increased) and take-home pay did not increase.

In summer of 1940 we started observing groups of refugees passing daily through the Novosibirsk station. These refugees came from the same places we had. Whenever we had time we would go to the station looking for relatives or friends. These refugees were not as free as we were when we arrived in Novosibirsk. What happened, why, and for what are they being punished? We learned that most of them registered to go back to German-occupied Poland. The secret police assembled them, and instead of sending the groups west they sent them to distant areas in the Soviet Union. Since such groups passed through Novosibirsk for several weeks, we surmised that there were many thousands of such exiles. As I learned later, their working and living conditions were much worse than ours, and most of them were freed only after the war. Yet most of them survived the war, avoiding a sure extinction under the Nazis in Poland.

One day I overheard a broadcast with Kusevitsky singing an aria with the Tbilisi Opera of Georgia. So Moshe Kusevitsky, the famous cantor from Tlomackie Synagogue in Warsaw, was in the Soviet Union? I was overwhelmed. My heart started pounding, and tears wet my eyes. It was as if I had met a dear friend from my childhood. Years later I learned that the Germans arrested him in 1939, but thanks to the effort of Polish artistic luminaries who managed to bribe the appropriate authorities, he was released and subsequently escaped to the Soviet side.

Overall our first months in Novosibirsk were a mixed bag. On one hand the authorities tried to create favorable conditions for us far exceeding those available to the Russian people. On the other hand we witnessed the miserable situation and careless treatment of the local population. It was not difficult to infer that we might also be treated like them after a short period of privilege. Most frightening was the evidence that the secret police had absolute power to use at will.

Invariably in our conversations we turned to the plight of our loved ones left under German occupation. From time to time, we got letters from them that didn't reveal too much about their real situation, but reading between the lines we understood that their life was much more difficult than ours. And we were unable to help them.

6
The Prosecutor's Case

My prospects of becoming a carpenter grew slimmer with each month of "training." Our instructor spent most of the time in the men's room, where he could smoke his pipe and tell stories. We, the trainees, had to produce a very primitive drying frame for the brick plant. We repeated the same tedious production of those simple frames for many months.

In the spring of 1941 I became fed up with the whole arrangement and decided to complain to the city prosecutor's office. The prosecutor was a friendly, nicely dressed woman of middle age. I told her that we were not learning anything useful despite so many months spent in what was supposed to be training. She met me with great warmth and sympathy, promising the office would look into the matter and give me an answer at my next visit within a few weeks. I was proud of myself and was convinced that I did the right thing. I could not understand why the government would tolerate such a waste of time and money.

On my next visit the same prosecutor, previously so friendly, met me with fierce hostility. She jumped at me from the moment I opened the door. "You German fascist! You came here to spread Nazi propaganda. Get out of here!" she yelled. I was perplexed. I couldn't understand what happened. I could be called all kinds of names, but clearly I was not a Nazi or a fascist. Why such change of attitude? When she calmed down a little, she asked me whether it was true that I gouged swastikas on pieces of wood in the shop. Aha, there it was! It was true; I did it without any particular aim when I was bored. It was a bad habit that many kids used to have during the prewar years in Poland. It was the same with any time-filling doodle, except that this particular symbol was the one most often emerging from the thoughtless use of a pencil, or in my case, a chisel. Maybe it was because it was such a forbidden and frightening mark that kids were attracted to it. I tried to explain this to the prosecutor, but to no avail. She kept hollering and finally ordered me out of her office.

Between my first and second visits she had obviously gotten in touch with the management of the carpentry shop. My instructor, who knew of the doodling, looked for a way out for himself, and I had given him a golden opportunity by once chiseling a swastika on a piece of wood that was too small to be used for anything except burning. He grabbed that piece of wood from me, led me into the manager's office, and charged that all I was doing was carving swastikas on our output, which was then sent to the brick plant, and in this way, I was spreading Nazi propaganda. The prosecutor quite naturally took the management's position and kicked me out of her office. I lost my case.

Worse, I had gotten myself into a very dangerous situation. I should have paid more attention to the stories my friend used to tell about the persecution of innocent people. In my case the prosecutor had proof of an activity that could easily be reported to the NKVD, and a ten-year sentence in a labor camp could result. Or the prosecutor herself could have punished me. None of this happened, and I wonder why. The best answer I can come up with was that the prosecutor took the risk of throwing out the evidence against me, as if it had never happened. I am very thankful for her understanding and magnanimity. I came to this conclusion based on my observation of the Russian people, whom I found sympathetic and willing to forgive. The woman gave the impression of a very warm, caring person. Part of her duties was to protect people who were wrongly accused—but only when it did not involve the government or the party. In my case, since I complained about a low-level civilian manager, who was in her eyes not fulfilling his obligations as an instructor, I am sure she quashed the whole matter.

This episode was only the beginning of my troubles with law enforcement authorities in the Soviet Union. Lack of perspective, low earnings, and the possibility of making more money elsewhere turned my attention to speculation—an activity forbidden in the Soviet Union. Since we Belorussians could buy items that were in short supply without standing in line for many hours or even days, we could easily resell them at a profit. There were not many such items, but I could buy a suit, a sweater, cloth, or boots. I did this a couple of times and was not caught.

My problem lay elsewhere. In 1939 or 1940, a law was promulgated in the Soviet Union that introduced stiff penalties for absenteeism or tardiness at work. The penalty for arriving more than twenty minutes late to work three times was a deduction of 15 to 25 percent from wages. For being absent several days, the penalty was imprisonment between three to six months. In order to buy goods for resale, I had to be near the department stores in the downtown area, not in the carpentry shop. I took some time off and was charged with absenteeism by the organization.

A judge and two jurors adjudicated my case. The jurors were selected from the general public and served for a few weeks, participating in all cases brought before a given judge or court. The jurors had practically nothing to say about guilt or innocence. Customarily the judge would explain the law and what the verdict should be to the jurors. I surmise that in cases without political implications some discussions in chambers usually took place. My case was heard in a courtroom in the presence of a young female judge and two jurors, also young women. The first question was my name and date of birth. Since it was now 1941, and I was at that time almost sixteen years old, I decided to tell them that I was recorded as having been born in 1923, but actually I was born in 1925. The court accepted my explanation without further question. I admitted that I hadn't shown up for work for several days, and at the same time expounded on why I was disappointed with the place I was working. That was all.

After a brief recess, I was called back into the chamber. The verdict was announced by the judge: Not guilty, because I was still a minor, less than sixteen years old, and the law didn't apply to minors. I was surprised because I thought they might consider my having lied about age as an additional criminal act. I was happy!

About a fortnight later, I was summoned again to a different court, where my case was reconsidered. It turned out that a higher-level appellate court rejected the verdict and sent the case back for reconsideration. The same procedure was followed as in the previous court. I stated the facts, including the inaccuracy of my birth date. The verdict was the same: Not guilty!

That was still not the end of it. Several weeks later I was charged again with the same absenteeism. This review rejected the earlier verdict on the basis that, as a minor, I could not be imprisoned for missing a few days of work, but there was no justification for letting me go scot-free. Therefore I should pay a fine. The verdict this time was that 25 percent of my miserable earnings should be deducted for three months.

However, the government could not collect that fine. It was already late spring, and our contract to work in Novosibirsk expired. We had learned from friends that in Ivanovo-Vozniesiensk, a city located in the European part of the USSR, food supplies were much better than elsewhere. Sam and I decided several months earlier that we would try to move to Ivanovo as soon as possible.

Two important formalities had to be taken care of. First, we needed a document that would entitle us to travel. The authorities offered all "liberated Belorussians" and "liberated Ukrainians" Soviet citizenship. Many refugees from Poland were reluctant to accept it, fearful that it might prevent them from ever returning to Poland. Many were counting on some turn of history that would allow them to return home after the defeated Germans left the country. Despite that risk Sam and I decided to accept the new citizenship and its passport, which allowed us to travel within the Soviet Union. Somehow, we believed that when the occupation of our homeland ended, conditions would be so different that we would be able to return to Poland. In the meanwhile we gained some freedoms and avoided a lot of trouble that those who rejected that offer had to endure, including being jailed for minor transgressions. Rejecting the offer of Soviet citizenship could be considered as the act of an enemy of the Soviet Union, with all the negative consequences.

The second formality was to get train tickets, a very difficult task. Somehow my brother acquired the tickets, and we disappeared from Novosibirsk.

7
Ivanovo-Vozniesiensk
Where One Could Buy Flour and Sugar

Each roommate in our Novosibirsk dormitory had his own special topic of conversation. One was paranoid about the persecution of innocent people. Others talked of their efforts to get a job in a garment factory. Still others spoke of their hope to return to Poland after the Germans left our homeland. Mendel often changed the conversation to the help he was going to get from his influential uncle in Moscow. When we left Novosibirsk, he asked us to visit his uncle and tell him about his plight and desire to go to Moscow. We were glad to promise to try.

The journey back to Europe was much more pleasant than the one to Siberia. We got tickets on the coach car of the Moscow-Vladivostok train. The entire journey lasted only four days. The weather was pleasant, since it was May, and I considered the trip a nice birthday gift. Through the windows we observed the landscape, the villages and little towns as well as the magnificent panorama of the Ural Mountains. The winter snow was finally melting, exposing the black soil to the sun's warmth. As we got closer to Europe, trees were blooming, tractors were plowing, and there were more people working in the fields. Most of the village houses we passed were log huts, the older ones sinking in the soil, certifying their durability. The stops in large cities were long enough to allow us to leave the train, mingle with people, buy some *pierozhki* (dumplings) from women on the platforms, or visit the bars inside the *vokzal* (station).

In Moscow, we had to change trains. We decided to look for Mendel's uncle and do a little sightseeing. The uncle lived on Sadovo-Tchernogradskaya Boulevard. It took us many hours of walking along boulevards that all were called Sadovo. Each time we asked directions to Sadovo-Tchernogradskaya, the answer was "further ahead." It turned out that Sadovo Boulevard formed a circle around the city, and various portions had different names added to identify the neighborhood. Ultimately, we found the place.

Initially, those in the apartment didn't want to let us in. They weren't sure that we were truly messengers from their nephew in Novosibirsk. Eventually we were able to convince them. It turned out that the uncle was not there; where he was, they wouldn't say. At first, they were afraid to talk about him, but after a while we were told that the uncle had been arrested, among the many persecuted by Stalin in the late 1930s. It was a depressing visit, and we were sorry for our friend in Novosibirsk, whose hopes would be dashed by our discovery. His relatives didn't want to ruin his dreams, or perhaps to admit their troubles, and that was why they had not informed him about his uncle's true situation. After this, we went sightseeing to several of the famous places in Moscow: Red Square near the Kremlin, the Bolshoi Theater, and the Lenin Mausoleum. Late in the afternoon we departed for Ivanovo, the last and relatively short leg on our journey from Siberia.

In Ivanovo, we rented a room in a single-family house #4 on the street named Seventeenth Lane, not far from a furniture factory, where I got a job as a carpenter. Sam was employed in a large textile mill, and both of us started a new life. The job in the furniture factory was relatively simple: assembling frames for mattresses and sofas. I had to prepare the glue, put it on the grooved boards, and then assemble the frame. It was a repetitive job that had to be done fast. The master carpenter under whom I worked was an alcoholic. When he was able to get vodka, a difficult task indeed at that time, he would not come to work for days. Yet the factory did not prosecute him, because he was a good worker when sober.

At a nearby section in the carpentry shop, a small team of three or four workers was binding mattresses and sofas and upholstering them. The chief specialist of the group was a Polish communist who had arrived at the end of 1939. He was a handsome man in his late forties, with light blond hair, a mustache, and light bluish eyes—resembling the *szlachcic* (nobleman) ideal that I knew from pictures. How could he be a communist? After a few weeks in the factory, I was offered a job in his section. I gladly accepted, and began to learn upholstery. I found that I liked it and learned pretty fast. Everything seemed to be working out for us. Our wages were not great, but were much better than in Novosibirsk. We could buy flour and sugar and other food and maintain a reasonable standard of living.

For the first time I was working in a place where many young women were also employed. I was not yet interested in getting involved with girls, at least not in the workplace. But others were freely flirting with them, especially during the lunch break. I was puzzled to see how willingly the girls let themselves be cuddled and thrown on mattresses, laughingly encouraging the contact with men (and not necessarily only the young or unmarried). It seemed innocent yet clearly involved contact with all the interesting parts of their bodies. It was a surprise to me, quite different from the relations between the sexes I was accustomed to in Poland, and only later did I understand this behavior was normal in the Soviet Union. A war, albeit a limited one, was still going on with Finland in 1940, and the Soviet Union sustained relatively high casualties. The persecution of its population in the 1930s had also reduced the male population, as did the military draft. It all combined to create an imbalance between the sexes, with many more females in the population. Therefore the women in our shop, and in many other places, were eager to flirt and permit caresses for the little pleasure they could derive from such play, even in public.

All the time we were in the Soviet Union, we corresponded with our parents. They spoke circumspectly of their lives out of fear of the German censors. Yet we knew of their general situation. At the end of the winter of 1940 they left Lodz and moved to Kamiensk, the little town where my mother's parents lived. Presumably, they hoped that nearby friendly farmers could provide them with food in exchange for goods or services. During that trip in a horse cart, Father suffered severe frostbite and fell so ill that he required hospitalization. He was operated on, although we did not learn for what, and there were complications that required a further hospital stay in the nearby town of Radomsko. We surmised that in the summer of 1940 Jews in Kamiensk and Radomsko were not yet confined to ghettos. My younger sister and brother were with our parents. Esther, my oldest unmarried sister, was working in a manor in a nearby village. Dvojra, my older sister, went to Tomaszow Mazowiecki, where she stayed with the Goldbergs, my father's relatives. I seem to remember letters that reached us later did have the stamp of Rumkowski—*Der Aelteste der Juden* (The Leader of the Jews)—in Litzmannstadt, a new name given the city of Lodz. However, from their last letter, which we got on June 18, 1941, I learned that my parents were still in Kamiensk. It is possible that they had to send mail through the ghetto in Lodz.

A few days after we received the last letter from our parents, war struck again, this time between the Soviet Union and Germany. Despite their nonaggression pact, Germany attacked on June 22, 1941. It was a very nice, sunny day. I was walking home from downtown Ivanovo when I heard the first war news over the radio. Now life for everyone in the Soviet Union would change dramatically. And with those changes, new opportunities would emerge to achieve my goal of fighting the Nazis. This development might provide the best chance to rescue my parents and relatives. But instead of good news from the front lines, reports were rather grim. The highly praised Red Army was retreating. The German blitzkrieg was succeeding in the Soviet Union, as it had in many countries before.

Within a few weeks, life in the furniture shop changed dramatically. Preparations were being made to transform the plant into war production. In the last two weeks before the war, a team of engineers arrived to build a prototype of a vehicle that would run on an airplane motor mounted at the back of a wooden cabin-like sleigh set on two broad skis. They had less trouble with the wooden parts than with the motor, which required many attempts before they finally succeeded in getting it to operate. We were told that the vehicle would be used to evacuate wounded soldiers from snow or ice-covered battlefields. It's likely that it was designed as a result of the Red Army's experience in the Finland war.

We stopped producing furniture and switched to making boxes for artillery shells. Within a few weeks, all men able to carry arms were mobilized for military duty. Only the very young, like me, or old men, and women remained in the plant. Remaining workers were divided into two 12-hour shifts, and ordered to increase production as much as possible. The atmosphere was sober, fewer workers were seen moving around the plant, and productivity increased. The workers understood the importance of getting the artillery shells to the front. I was initially transferred to work on the assembly line; some months later, I became the operator of a big machine that looked like a tank. Conveyers moved on different levels, simultaneously cutting lengths of wood, drilling holes, and scoring grooves. Before the war only the most experienced technicians operated that huge machine. I didn't know how to run it properly, but the daughter of the former chief technician Gerasimov was sent to train me. I found that I could operate the machine easily. At first it was even fun. The big machine made the pieces and worked well. The smaller finishing machines, and especially the assembly of the artillery boxes, was done mostly by hand, and that limited output. Therefore workers from other sections, including me, were often sent to help in assembling the boxes.

Twelve-hour shifts and insufficient food affected our strength. But we were still young and didn't mind working hard to defeat the Nazis. Our daily ration of 800 grams of bread was higher than the 600 grams given those working in the civilian economy. Elderly nonworking citizens and children got only 400 grams. I remember that we also got a pound of sugar and a similar amount of meat per month. Wages were still low, and the price of a loaf of bread was about 100 to 150 rubles on the market, equivalent to two weeks' work. But the ration system functioned well: all the time I was in Ivanovo, until the spring of 1942, the supply system worked without interruption.

Late in the fall of 1941, Comrade Koshelev, the chief engineer and head of the Communist Party cell, called an emergency meeting. His message was grim and worrisome: we might fall under German occupation at any moment. The Germans were nearing Moscow. Koshelev told us that the German tactics consisted of an onslaught of large tank units, moving ahead at top speed if they did not encounter any resistance, and stopping only when they ran out of fuel—usually some 140 kilometers. When they reached their objective, airborne units parachuted in and occupied the place. Then army units moved in and mopped up any remaining resistance. Since Ivanovo was about 300 kilometers east of Moscow, it was possible that in a few days we might find ourselves under German occupation. Therefore, the authorities decided to distribute all valuable materials from the textile mills and warehouses among the general population to prevent the goods from falling into the hands of the enemy. Anyone could have a large amount of material without charge, just for a signature. Ivanovo fell into a frenzy. Hundreds of people carried huge bundles of cloth from the textile factories through the streets, as the city prepared for possible occupation. Party members and officials got ready to evacuate or join the underground. Columns of elderly men in the *Narodnoye Opoltshenye* (local defense units) marched back and forth, holding wooden *vintovcas* (rifles) and singing the ominous military song: *Idiot voina narodnaya, sviaschennaya voina* (the people's holy war is underway). It went on, "Raise our great land for the deadly battle." These were not actual fighting units. They were only training basic marching movements for which the authorities did not want to provide real rifles.

The atmosphere felt loaded with fear and apprehension. It was a surreal mixture of near panic balanced by a stern determination to resist as exemplified by those units marching with wooden rifles. Was the Soviet Union succumbing to the might of Hitler's army or did it have the inner strength, not yet revealed, to throw back the invaders, as had happened many times in its history? I didn't know the answer to that, and I also worried that I might again fall into the hands of the Nazis. This time there was no possibility of escape; the factory was running without interruption. I had to stay put and hope for the best.

Soon thereafter the situation on the front started improving. The Red Army finally stopped the German offensive at the outskirts of Moscow. Instead of moving ahead deeper into the cold, the Nazis tried to consolidate their gains. They had met "General Moroz," the Russian winter, and had to concentrate on surviving. The Russians, on the other hand, were used to the freezing weather and used the opportunity to assemble overwhelming power, mobilizing units from Siberia. Not only did they stop the advancing German military machine, they launched successful counterattacks, pushing the Germans back and away from Moscow. The danger of my falling in German hands again faded, at least for the time being.

At the start of the Soviet-German war the period of my adjustment to life in the Soviet Union came to an abrupt end. I had transformed over the last year and a half. From a Jewish boy raised in a religious family that honored the faith and followed its precepts, I entered a life void of any religious content in a country that fiercely pursued the eradication of all religions except Communism. I ceased to use the languages of my childhood—Hebrew, Yiddish, and Polish—and switched to Russian. From a naïve believer in the pursuit of justice I became a skeptic. I had trouble adopting the Russian maxim: *Snachala bylo trudno potom pryvykniesh, nitchevo* (Initially it is hard, but after you get used to it, it's OK). One had to get used to a situation, but I was slow to learn that, as I was still rebellious, which caused me trouble. It was a time of danger and sheer luck, of peril and good fortune.

When the Soviet-German war broke out in 1941 my future became even more unpredictable, but I reached a clear determination on what I wanted to do. My instinct for rebellion sparked a burning desire to return to my country on a Russian tank and to liberate my family and people. I decided to leave the relative secure walls of the furniture factory for the open and dangerous battlefield. I promised myself that I would fight the Nazis at any cost.

2
My War with the Nazis

8

The Working Battalions of the Red Army

In the spring of 1942, I volunteered for the Red Army. It was my hope that, after enlisting and a short training period, I would join the struggle against the Germans. Unfortunately, a strange number, 37, marked my Soviet identity document. It indicated that I was a foreigner who didn't have all the rights of a native citizen. In this particular case, it meant that the authorities would not trust me in the Red Army. Instead, I was sent to the "Working Battalions," which were under the authority of the General Management of Airfield Construction (GUAS in Russian).

The GUAS battalions were building airfields close to the front lines. From these fields, tactical airplanes would rise to support advancing units or assist in defense against German offensives. The airfields were also used for long-distance air strikes: planes would take off at sunset and return after a long-range mission at dawn the next day. In winter GUAS units serviced the snow-covered airfields so that bombers could take off on long-range night missions.

Our winter routine was as follows: We would get up early in the morning, at five o'clock, and march for about an hour toward the airfield. Sometimes we lost our way as blowing snow completely covered the narrow paths leading to the airfield. To our surprise, often we would end up in the middle of the runway. When that happened, soldiers would fire red rockets to let us know we were in the wrong (and dangerous) place, since this was also the time the bombers would land after their night missions. After arriving at the huge mess hall, we would stand in line for hot soup and a piece of bread. The soup was usually very thin, reflecting the food supply problems that struck after the Germans occupied most of the Ukraine, the breadbasket of the Soviet Union. After breakfast, we shoveled snow to clear the center of the airfields.

It was extremely cold, and we were freezing. By evening we would reassemble in the kitchen to get more soup or porridge and then march back to the village where we were quartered.

We didn't have any weapons, and our military training was minimal—just enough to march in columns and perform basic turns. Nevertheless, the unit commanders tried to maintain some semblance of military discipline, but with very meager results. The units were made up of a variety of human material—first were the foreigners. Even though a few years earlier we were considered "liberated Belorussians," now we were at best second-class citizens, not trusted to bear arms in the struggle against the invaders. Then there were people who had been jailed on the basis of the famous paragraph 58 of the criminal code for counterrevolutionary activity. They had served their sentences and were now technically free. There were also sons and close relatives of those considered "enemies of the people"—persons the regime accused of antigovernment activity. Not only were they sent away to labor camps, but their relatives fell under suspicion also and were not accepted in the regular army. A significant part of GUAS personnel were therefore experienced labor camp prisoners who knew the life and order of the labor camps very well. Indeed, our units often worked side by side with prisoners from the infamous gulags.

For most of the winter of 1942 our battalion was spread out and housed in villages about three to four miles from an airfield. In the house where I was billeted, about thirty GUAS soldiers slept in two levels of bunks. Understandably, the air inside the room was not of the best quality. Even more of a nuisance were the nightly games of blackjack in which a large number of soldiers participated. The stakes were very rich, for real money or other valuables. Several times during the night a quarrel would erupt with shouting often leading to a fistfight. The participants in those games were experienced former gulag prisoners, who tried any subterfuge to avoid getting up in the morning for work. They knew, for example, how to develop high fevers, enabling them to stay in their quarters and still get a daily ration of food. However, for one reason or another the rations for those who were unable or unwilling to go to work did not always arrive, and after a prolonged period of missing out on regular food, they got increasingly weaker and became truly unable to work. Such soldiers were called "*dokhodiaga*" meaning "approaching the end."

In the spring and summer of 1943 we were often transferred frequently, roughly following the situation on the front. In one such transfer I met my brother Sam, who had been mobilized and assigned to a battalion similar to mine. We were happy to see each other, but unfortunately it lasted only a few weeks. Sam saw me physically grown up and well adapted to military life. We tried to be together as much as possible, exchanging stories of our experiences while separated, and we spoke often about our loved ones left behind under German occupation. While he was still a civilian Sam had a better opportunity to learn something about the situation of Jews in Poland, which we heard was extremely difficult, but we did not yet know about the murderous death camps. Living together lifted our spirits and raised hope for future meetings. Sam was then sent to the northern region of the USSR where working conditions were much harsher than mine.

We were housed with the local population, and as the villages were organized in collective farms, their inhabitants depended on the food supplied from the *kolkhoz*. Unless they worked for an enterprise or an institution outside the farm, village residents did not receive the rations of bread and other items that urban dwellers were entitled to. I shared my ration of bread with the family that hosted me, while they contributed potatoes to our common meals.

Despite the difficult war conditions and unrelenting hard work, the young girls in the village would assemble in the evening for dancing and singing. The typical songs were the *ciastushki*—rhyming couplets poking fun at the improper behavior of boys, praising true love, or mocking human weakness. Most of them reflected real life in a humorous way. Each couplet was accompanied by associated tunes played on a *garmoshka* (accordion) and provoked laughter among the listeners. The music was also accompanying the dances of which the Russians are masters. They practiced a much more elaborate tap dancing than I have ever seen elsewhere. Russian folk tradition at its best was preserved during the war, even though the news from the battlefields was not always cheerful. What I saw of life in a Russian village I witnessed when the Soviets already halted the advance of the Germans, about a year after the victory of Stalingrad and the turning of the tide in the famous battle of Kursk in the summer of 1943. I was told that even in the worst of times Russian youths did not lose hope and the singing and dancing relieved anxieties and stress and kept morale high.

In the summer of 1943, my unit was assigned to work in a quarry. It was a surface quarry of little pebbles, which we shipped to a site of a future airfield. I was a member of a "*udarnaya brygada*"—meaning that our team worked very hard to load the pebbles at record speed. We removed the topsoil from little hills under which pebbles were loose and ready to be picked up and loaded on three-ton trucks. I loaded pebbles with a large, wide shovel for six to seven hours without a break. The trucks approached the loading site, one after the other, as on a conveyer belt. There was no time for a rest or to light a cigarette. During those six or seven hours our crew produced three times the amount established as the norm. As a reward, we could knock off before the formal end of the shift, and every member of the team got an extra portion of soup.

However, the pace and difficulty of this kind of work affected my health. I experienced chest pain and abnormal heartbeat; doctors were not sure what it meant. After several visits, the doctors directed that I leave the shovel crew and be transferred to another job. So late in the summer of 1943, my new job was to operate four excavating shovels, each the capacity of a cubic yard, which were attached to a heavy tractor. After several weeks of lifting the handles of the four containers, a tumor developed under my left arm, which sent me to a military hospital. Since we worked for the air force, the hospital had a large contingent of airmen wounded in action.

As soon as I entered the hospital I could see the terrible results of the war. I passed an open room where on a table I saw a severely wounded man without his legs, bleeding from the stumps of his remaining thighs, which were jerking up and down in agony. This sight shocked me deeply. It was the first time that I witnessed such severe wounds or someone so close to death. The wounded man was left unattended and I could not understand why. Later I understood when I observed that the emergency room had to deal with large numbers of wounded arriving simultaneously and who could not be taken care of immediately. The surgeons made quick selections, and the one wounded man whom I saw was not chosen for immediate care. Nurses gave the wounded a drink of red wine, which was thought to strengthen them and make it a little easier to bear the pain.

In the big ward where I was given a bed, there were probably one hundred beds crammed close together, full of severely wounded servicemen. The odor from their wounds was terrible. Some were without legs or hands, or with severe wounds on their bodies, and many were screaming, begging to be killed, to end the unbearable pain and suffering. In the following days I often heard men begging the nurses, "*sestritchka dobiej menia*" (sister, please finish me off). The nurses would say something comforting to them and continue taking care of others. I can only imagine how difficult it was for these young girls to cope in that dreadful job. Night was the worst time. I lay listening to the screaming and smelling the odor and could only sympathize with the wounded. They were in the hands of the medical team that did its best. Unfortunately, some of the severely wounded would not survive.

The shock of the hospital experience should have caused me to pause and think again about what I was doing, why I was trying so hard to join the fight. Wouldn't it be better to stay in the labor battalions where there was no danger of being killed or wounded? If such thoughts entered my mind I dismissed them as fast as they tried to derail my plan to join the fight against the Nazis. My internal drive was not deflected by any thought of possible death or injury. I think that most, if not all, soldiers do not join a battle thinking they will be killed. It is the only reason that soldiers can keep fighting when fear could paralyze their actions. My decision was firm. I was determined to realize my plan of joining the Red Army.

My medical problem was relatively simple compared to many others. In a few days, a physician had looked at my tumor, diagnosed it as not malignant, and promised that within three weeks I would be back in good shape. He was right; the medication he applied worked and my tumor started shrinking.

Since my legs were healthy, the hospital assigned me to assist in serving food to the wounded who had to stay in bed. This gave me a lot of contact with pilots and other airmen, many of them officers. They told combat stories; frequent were stories about the poor combat record of soldiers from *natzmens* (national minorities): Muslims, for example, would assemble around a killed comrade in the middle of the battle and pray. Minority soldiers were poorly disciplined, and the Russian commanders of such units had a lot of trouble accomplishing their missions.

When not helping with meals, I was assigned as an aide to a military prosecutor with the rank of captain. Since it was an evacuation hospital it had to be located close to the front lines. As the front moved, so did the hospital. The captain prosecutor was sent to the hospital to investigate, to my mind, a rather trivial case of the disappearance of several gallons of wine that the hospital was supposed to use for severely wounded servicemen. My task was to stay by the door in the room where the investigation took place and call in some physician or administrator whenever the captain decided to confront the current interviewee with other witnesses. Since I had been in the hospital for several weeks and moved around frequently, I knew many of the personnel and where to find them. The investigation always took place at night. The principal suspect was the director of the hospital, a man in his sixties. At about two o'clock in the morning, he would beg to end the interrogation for the day, since he was very tired and no longer knew what he was saying. The captain would, most of the time, satisfy his request, be very polite, and ask me to accompany the hospital director to his quarters.

My impression was that the prosecutor really didn't have a case strong enough to continue the investigation for so many days. However, the captain was not in a hurry; the position he was in was very comfortable, and clearly he was not looking for other assignments. And although he was accusing the hospital director of illegally diverting some hospital wine, the captain would send me to a "friendly" woman in a regional military supply warehouse with a list of food and drink she was to send to him. But he was an amiable man, willing to share the good food with me.

My goal, however, was not to stay in the hospital. I wanted to be sent to a regular unit of the Red Army. For this reason, when I registered at the hospital, I made sure that I was considered as a regular soldier of the Red Army. My uniform, of course, testified that this was true. At the hospital admission desk they didn't make any attempt to check any documents; actually I don't think I had any.

Upon my release from the hospital, I made sure that I was dispatched to a regular Red Army replacement unit, as was done with any wounded serviceman released from the hospital and medically able to go back to a regular army unit. My efforts to outwit the system had worked; I was now sure that I would be able to join the regular army and get a rifle in my hands. My good luck struck again!

9
In the Eighth Reserve Regiment of the Red Army

Shortly after I arrived at the headquarters of the Eighth Reserve Regiment of the Red Army, near Rzhev in a place called Zapadnaya Dvina, a sergeant read us an order that soldiers of Polish origin be sent to a Polish army then being formed. At first, we called this Polish army the Wanda Wasilewska Army, after the Polish communist leader authorized by Stalin to undertake its formation. This force was also known as the Kosciuszko Army and the Berling Army (from its commander, General Zygmunt Berling). I preferred to think of it under the name of the Polish hero, referred to it as the Kosciuszko Army.

I had to think quickly. The first thought that came to my mind was of the many Polish Jews in the GUAS Battalion who dreamed of joining a Polish army previously formed in the USSR, the Anders Army. They wanted to enter the war in a more direct and meaningful way, but could not realize that dream. Now I had such an opportunity. My immediate inclination was to say yes, I am from Poland. Service with the Kosciuszko force had the additional advantage that participation of the liberation of Poland was promised, and that might not be the case for those serving in the regular Soviet army.

For several weeks I participated in regular training in the Eighth Reserve Regiment of the Red Army. I was assigned to a sapper (engineering) unit, whose task was fording rivers or building temporary bridges across them, and laying mines for defense or clearing minefields before advancing units. This is very dangerous combat service, but in training there was no serious suffering. It was still early fall 1943, the weather was mild, and I even enjoyed being there. The food was much better than in the working battalions, and the real soldiers were delightful companions, especially in the evenings after the daily training. I would often be sent to the kitchen to carry the daily ration of bread, sugar, and hot food to the barracks. The procedure for dividing the bread and sugar was well established and very elaborate in order to be fair to everybody. The most senior sergeant performed that important task, and there was never any complaint. After soldiers had their meals in the evening, they would lie down on their bunks, 150 to 200 in all, and sing. I recall the very touching war song: "*O Dniepro, Dniepro, Ty Sherok Moguch, Nad Toboy Letiat Zhuravli*" ("Oh Dniepr, Wide, Magnificent Dniepr, Cranes Are Flying over You"). Those were the most joyful and memorable moments of my service in the Red Army. I was very happy among these troops and felt comfortable serving with them as my Russian conversation skills were near perfect. The drawback was that these new friendships could not last long, as soldiers were scattered among fighting units after a very short stay in the reserve regiment.

While my comrades were singing, memory carried me back to the music of my childhood. In my head resounded melodies sung during prayers by the Wolborska Synagogue choir. I thought of Moshe Kusevitsky, the phenomenal performer of liturgical music and famous cantor from the Tlomackie Synagogue in Warsaw. In the fall of 1938, Kusevitsky gave a concert at the Philharmonic Hall in Lodz, which I was lucky enough to attend thanks to my brother Samuel. Kusevitsky's singing of the prayers were so much better than anything I had known in Hebrew liturgical music, and I was immensely moved by them. I couldn't imagine that a mere human could have such a strong and beautiful tenor voice, able to phrase dramatic melodies with such ease and clarity. Above all, I recalled the sweetness of his voice and the emotional power of the music that reached deep into the Jewish soul. The memory of how I felt when I heard Kusevitsky became a force that helped sustain me in the excruciating difficulties that were to come.

The Rebbe from Tomaszow was another source of musical influence. My paternal grandfather Simon was his close disciple. On each visit the Rebbe would invite my father and me into his study and inquire about my father's business and my progress in learning the Torah. The prayers at the Tomaszower Rebbe's services were memorable because of their authenticity, sincerity, and dramatic power. I recall the Yom Kippur prayers, which are always intense and dramatic since Jews are asking to be released from unfulfilled promises they have made to God as well as for forgiveness of their transgressions. The Tomaszower Rebbe's prayers were extraordinary, and I was led to believe that he communicated directly with God. The Rebbe sang his prayers as a soloist accompanied by a choir. His velvety bass was absolutely convincing in his dramatic appeals to God. He carried the worshipers with him as he approached the Almighty. In the middle of a song he would suddenly stop. It would then be very quiet. I had the feeling that, maybe now, the heavens had opened and heard his, and therefore our, prayers.

I realized, in the Red Army barracks, how much my world of traditional words and songs had changed. These two worlds differed so much, and in a way they were the opposites of each other. Religious poetry compared with secular; the Hebrew and the Russian languages; extolling God or the beauty of nature; heaven or earth; peace opposing war. Despite all the differences they engendered the same feelings of nobility, emotion, and awareness of the sublime. Music and poetry are truly universal.

Like many others in this reserve unit, my goal was not to remain forever. The fortunes of the Red Army had improved greatly by that time, and kicking the Germans out of Soviet territory was now a real possibility. Joining the fighting units would open for me the chance of participating in the liberation of Poland, and with a little luck, I might even come back a victor to save my parents and siblings.

Several weeks passed and I continued practicing how to lay mines, while others were sent out to fight. My suspicions grew that something was wrong. The sergeant who met us when we arrived at the regiment was also being held longer than the others, despite his good health and perfect credentials. What was the matter with him? There were a few more reservists also being held without explanation. Finally, the sergeant learned from friends at regimental headquarters what the problem was. He came over one evening, after consuming a larger than usual dose of vodka, swearing fiercely that he was a member of the *Komsomol* (Communist Youth League) in good standing, had always served his country, never deviated from the party line, and why did they discriminate against him? He wanted to go and fight!

He had learned that the military authorities decided that five of us reservists, who were either born in Poland or had Polish relatives, were not to be trusted in regular Red Army units. Unknowingly, the sergeant (who turned out to have a Polish grandmother) had lured us into a trap with the promise of serving in a Polish unit. All of us, he had learned, would be sent to Siberia to work in a coal mine. My well-laid plans, seemingly so successful, to serve in a combat force bound for Poland, had led instead to a sentence of forced labor, together with the sergeant who induced me to admit my Polish origin. What irony!

I was in utter desperation. Now not only would I not be able to fight the Nazis, but I would have to work in a coal mine in Siberia! And should I blame myself for admitting that I was from Poland? What could I do now, to whom could I appeal? I fell back to thoughts that there must be some mistake, that this verdict could be reversed. But I did not know how or by whom. For a few weeks, I hoped that perhaps the information from headquarters was wrong or inaccurate or would be changed. There were reasons for hope. In 1943, Wanda Wasilewska, head of the ZPP, *Zwiazek Patriotów Polskich* (Association of Polish Patriots), was received by Stalin and during that meeting it was agreed that a new Polish army would be formed under the management and control of Polish communists. Therefore, I hoped, the plans of the Eighth Reserve Regiment were based on obsolete orders and would be changed soon.

As a matter of fact, we were soon informed that we would indeed be sent to the new Polish army, and that a colonel would accompany us to the place of its formation, which we learned was not far from Moscow. The colonel would have all our documents and would be our commander on the way to the Polish Army. I was happy again. It seemed logical to me. But the sergeant didn't believe this story, and he planted doubt in my mind. We were given new Red Army winter uniforms with woolen boots (*valonki*) that reinforced our suspicion that these uniforms, especially the boots, were intended for a Siberian winter rather than for service in the Polish Army. In that army, soldiers never wore woolen boots, even in severe winters; we weren't familiar with such footwear.

Finally, the colonel assembled us and we departed, ostensibly to a place not far from Moscow, still insisting that we were going to the Polish Army. There were five of us. We were given rations and were sent off on a comfortable journey, this time in a regular coach car, first to Moscow and then on the Moscow-Vladivostok train. We told everyone that we were joining the Polish Army and were traveling to its formation. Not long after boarding the Moscow-Vladivostok train, some people told us that they had met a captain of the Polish Army traveling on the same train in a nearby coach car. We went immediately and found him in a luxury compartment. We saluted him in the Russian form and he responded with the *czolem*, the traditional Polish military greeting. He was very pleasant. We told him our story and the suspicions we had that we would not be released at the Polish Army's place of formation, but, rather, would continue on to Siberia. He pretended that he didn't believe this. He told us that he was traveling all over the Soviet Union on a mission to recruit Poles from workplaces and even detention. However, in the event that we weren't incorporated into the Polish Army, whose base was not far away, he gave us the address of Wanda Wasilewska, and said that she would certainly make sure that we would be sent to the proper place. This visit with a real Polish officer and hearing his promises raised our spirits, despite our fear that we were being taken against our will to Siberia. At least there was now hope that we could extricate ourselves, if necessary.

Our suspicions turned out to be correct. We continued our journey to Siberia. The same colonel was not ashamed to lie to us all the way. Our final destination turned out to be a coal mine in Kandalaki, part of the Trest Molotov Ugol, in the Kuznetsk Coal Basin.

This place was deeper in Siberia than Novosibirsk, the city where I had lived in 1940–41. I could easily imagine the frost during the eight months of winter and the huge and impassable puddles created when the ice and snow did melt. Novosibirsk was a big city with some attractions, but Kandalaki was a barren place. It was already winter there, everything was snow covered, hiding any possibly interesting feature. As soon as I stepped down from the train a fellow approached me and said that if they sent me to work down at the nearby coal field I would last no more than three months. If I were to work above ground, I would get a ration of only four hundred grams of bread and my prospects would not be much better.

Upon arriving, the colonel, carrying a thick packet of documents, went to the offices of the coal mine. I wondered what kind of documents he had on me. They could not have much information; I was only eighteen years old. They had had several months to assemble the documents, and I surmised that they didn't neglect any source of information. Didn't they have better things to do during this horrible war? They must have been at great pains to build a case that would justify sending me to this coal mine. I was sure they knew of my misbehavior in Novosibirsk.

I had these dismal thoughts for company while I waited the several hours until the colonel came out of the office with a verdict: soldier Abram Broner will stay here in the coal mine. Two or three others from the group were told that they would be sent to the Kosciuszko Army. This verdict was outrageous, and I decided I had to argue my case without delay.

First I went to a lieutenant in the office of the town's military commissar to appeal. I told him that I was from Poland and should be sent to the Polish Army, as the other soldiers were. His response was rude. "You are not Polish, you are a Jew and we are not sending the other soldiers to a Jewish Army." I responded, "But listen, I was born in Poland, in Lodz, in the part of Poland that has not been annexed to the Soviet Union; therefore, I should be treated as a Polish citizen. Please check my language; I speak Polish just like those other soldiers." My arguing did not convince him. His answer was the same: "You are Abram Broner, son of Israel. What are you talking about? You are Jewish and we won't send you to the Polish Army."

I decided to appeal to a higher authority. This time it was to the commissar himself, a Red Army major. I reported myself according to the rules of the Red Army, which I still served, and told him that I was young and should go to the front where the fighting was, because that was where the country needed me. I had changed my argument, thinking that it sounded patriotic and appropriate, and that he would not be able to reject this reasoning. "Yes," he said, "you are young, but the country needs you here. This is our second front, and the country needs coal." "Yes, true," I retorted. "But here you can use older people, women, those who cannot serve in the military. I belong in the fighting army." I thought that I had gotten to him. He couldn't find any suitable answer. Then he turned to threats. "You must immediately go to work. If you don't, we will arrest you. Now leave this room." My appeal was over, and I was crushed. I returned to my comrades who were to be sent back to the Polish Army. In the meantime, a few more had joined their group. Two were young men released from prison that same day. All five were very friendly fellows. They asked what I had decided to do. I said, "I am escaping. If you want me, I'll go with you." They asked, "But how?" I responded, "I will manage."

10
A Red Army Deserter from Siberia

I had to think fast if I was to escape safely. My journey on the Moscow-Vladivostok train had taught me how the railway system worked. And my scheme was as follows: I would go to the railway station and board the train as a helper for the female attendant, whose duties include heating the car and preparing tea for the passengers. There was a tiny heating unit in a compartment at the end of the car, which had a door that could be closed. An unsuspecting railway official, checking the tickets and travel documents, would have no reason to look into it.

But how could I get the girl to let me serve as her illegal assistant? The answer came immediately. I went up to her and said, "Look, you are getting a very limited supply of coal to heat your unit. I'll bring you a lot more coal if you'll let me ride to the next large city, Kemerovo." She agreed. Now I had to deliver. That was easy enough. There were hundreds of cars loaded with coal. All I had to do was to climb on top of a few cars and get coal in a way that would not be noticed. The tops of the coal cars were sprayed with white lime, so that any significant removal of coal would be detected. But I didn't worry about that, since we were scheduled to leave the station soon. Besides, it was nighttime and even in daylight the white paint was not visible from below. My only worry was being caught while removing the coal from the car or while carrying it to the heating compartment. Well, one always has to count on a little luck. And on that night, I was lucky.

While traveling to the next city, I had to think about the other tricks I would use to succeed in an escape of three thousand miles. The first leg of my escape went according to the plan. Yes, there were passenger inspections. The attendant was kind enough to close the door of the heating compart-

ment, and pretend that she was sweeping the vicinity of the heating compartment just as the railway official approached. And it worked thanks to that
brave Russian girl whose name I don't even know.

When we reached the next city, the group of five Poles had to report to a
military office, where they were given rations for the next leg of the journey
to Novosibirsk. A few more were added to the group, so now there were seven
travelers, six legal and one illegal. Among the new arrivals was Kazik, a young
Polish man from Warsaw, who was released from jail that same day. He was a
very down-to-earth fellow. "Yes," he said, "you can travel with us, but remember that you have to contribute some food to the group. You have to understand, the ration is not enough to share with you. We will divide it up, but
you must contribute something." And he gave me a lesson on how to do this.
"There are a lot of passengers traveling to prisons or army units or to relatives
and who have food with them. All you have to do is to remove some of it. It's
simple, understand?" Yes, for him it was simple. He knew how to do it; he had
experience, he was jailed for stealing. But I had never stolen anything (other
than the coal from the Kandalaki train station). However, I understood that
as much as I despised it, I must bring something. I had to stay with the group,
which was the only way to reach my destination.

On the way to Novosibirsk, where we had to change trains again, there
were now eight of us. A sergeant in our group was chosen to be *starshoy*
(leader). He held the documents for the seven legal travelers. He would sit at
one end of the car with a few soldiers from the group. At the other end of the
car a few more soldiers positioned themselves. The rest, including me, would
sit in the middle of the car. It was a natural arrangement, which allowed me
to move from place to place if necessary. Quite often, I chose to sleep under
the benches. There was always room there. Besides, maybe I could "acquire a
share" of food from an unsuspecting fellow traveler while I was under the
bench. Most of the time, when military or civilian officials came in, I was
sleeping under the bench. People would tell the inspector that a soldier was
there, and his leader was at the end of the car. They never bothered to ask me
to get out from under the bench. They never tried to add up all the heads in
the group to find out if there were more than the documents indicated.

On the train from Novosibirsk, we used the same procedure as above.
Moreover, I had already learned from experience when to expect a military
inspection. The Narodnyi Komissariat Vnutrennikh Del (NKVD, the People's
Commissariat for Internal Affairs) did the checking; they usually boarded the

train in a large city. The review of documents lasted several hours, and by the time we reached the next stop (usually some 125 miles), they would have finished and would then leave the train, so I could roughly guess when the inspectors would arrive in our car.

We had a few close calls, though. One time I sat with an NKVD general who was traveling with us the whole day. We chatted about the difficult life of soldiers and our destination—the Polish Army. The inspector who came by was very polite in the general's presence. I told them that I was going to the Polish Army, and that our leader had all the documents and was sitting at the end of the car. One day I lay under the bench, battling with my conscience. I did not want to steal, but reality required it. It took me a lot of sweating before I reached for the unattended food. I got a few *lepioshki* and *pieroshki* (bread sticks and dumplings), which satisfied that day's demand for my contribution.

Even though I was proud of my clever scheme to escape from the coal mine, looking back I have to admit that it was naïve and very dangerous. With a little effort the authorities could easily have found me, since I did not report to work in the coal mine and was not in the dormitory. The first place to look was among the group that was traveling to the Polish Army. Any conductor who had been alerted would have found me with them. Maybe they did not look for me. Was it lack of cooperation between the military and the NKVD, or just the inefficiencies of wartime? I can only guess. This was my second fortunate escape from Siberia in the span of two years.

The closer we came to our destination, the more I worried. I was sure that the Polish Army cooperated closely with Soviet authorities. And technically I was a deserter from the Red Army. The Polish authorities might not look favorably on a Soviet deserter trying to enlist in their army. And what if they had the same policy as the Soviet authorities at the coal mine, and considered themselves a purely Polish Army that Poles of Jewish origin had no right to join? The closer we got to Divovo, about one hundred miles southeast of Moscow, the more apprehensive I became.

We still had to change to a local train to get to Divovo. On that train, most of the travelers would be Poles heading to the Polish Army. My anxiety increased enormously as the hour of truth approached. I thought, "Either I'll make it, or I'll be returned to the Soviet authorities and punished for desertion."

The train finally stopped. Through the windows we saw men in Polish uniforms. We got off and were immediately met by a junior officer, who asked the newly arrived: "Who is without legal documents?" I looked around and saw a forest of hands in the air. So I too raised my hand, knowing that as far as documentation went I was safe. I did not register under the biblical name Abram; instead, I was now Adam Broner. Nobody knew, so nobody could question, my father's name Israel. I knew that from then on I would be a soldier in the Polish Army and that my real war would start! The first phase of my journey—to become a warrior and get a rifle in my hand—had been accomplished.

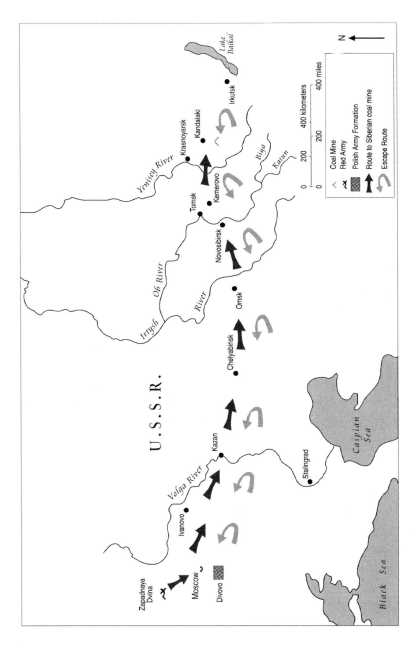

3. Deportation to and escape from a Siberian coal mine, 1943

11
Polish Armed Forces in the Soviet Union

The history of Poland during World War II is uniquely tragic. Poland was the first country attacked by the Germans, who brought the world to the precipice of subjugation to the most brutal regime humankind has ever known. Poland resisted heroically with great determination but inadequate means. Suffering defeat from the much better armed Germans, Poland was then invaded from the east by the Red Army, bringing its independence to an end. But the nation did not give up, and from the first month of occupation began its resistance. An underground resistance movement fought the Nazis throughout the entire occupation.

After the Red Army's occupation of eastern Poland on September 17, 1939, several hundred thousand Polish military personnel were captured and deported to labor camps and prisons in the Soviet gulag. In addition, during the years 1939–41, the Soviets conducted massive deportations of civilians from the annexed territories to Siberia and the Russian northeast.

When the Germans attacked the Soviet Union in June 1941, a new situation emerged, in which the Western countries that had been at war with Germany since September 1939 could organize a broader coalition of allies against the Nazis. But by then the German army occupied almost all Europe. The Polish government-in-exile in London sought an opportunity to build up its forces from refugees and prisoners scattered in other countries. It turned to the Soviet Union, where a huge reserve of Polish citizens could be mobilized to join the common goal of fighting and defeating the Germans.

On July 30, 1941, a Soviet-Polish pact was signed in London. It stipulated renewing diplomatic relations between the two countries, freeing Polish citizens held in prisons and labor camps, and the organization of a Polish Army in the Soviet Union. General Wladyslaw Anders, himself a prisoner held by the NKVD in the infamous Lubyanka prison, was named commander-in-chief of that army by the Polish government.

On August 14, 1941, a Polish-Soviet military agreement was signed, and two days later Gen. Anders had a meeting with General Aleksei Pavlovich Panfilov from the Soviet general staff, who indicated that only 20,000 Poles were in Soviet prisons and labor camps. That immediately raised suspicions about the whereabouts of the hundreds of thousands who had been interned by the Soviets in 1939. The Soviets wanted one Polish Division ready for combat by October 1, 1941. This was absolutely impossible. Moreover, Anders was opposed to sending one division into combat instead of the entire Polish Army. He reasoned that one unprepared and untrained division might be annihilated in the coming winter battles. Another concern was the survival of emaciated recruits who were former prison and labor-camp inmates, now assembled in bases in the Ural Mountains region, where they were quartered in small, snow-covered tents. More volunteers were arriving than the Soviets predicted, creating a problem in getting sufficient rations to them, as many came with their families. It was a constant struggle with the Soviet authorities, who limited the rations to a maximum of 44,000. Soldiers had to share rations with family members. There was privation everywhere. All these issues were raised in a meeting between Stalin, Molotov, and the representatives of the Polish government headed by its prime minister, General Wladyslaw Sikorski, with the participation of General Anders and Polish ambassador Stanislaw Kot. From his notes of that meeting, Anders reports in his 1981 memoir that Sikorski claimed: "A great number of our most valuable people are still in labor camps and prisons." Stalin replied: "That is impossible, because the amnesty applied to all Poles, and all Poles were released." Sikorski and Anders continued to claim that many thousands of missing officers were deported by the Soviets and had not been released. Stalin promised to issue instructions that all Poles were to be released. Then Sikorski raised another issue. He asserted that, "The conditions under which the Polish Army is now being organized are entirely inadequate. Soldiers are becoming frostbitten in the light tents; they suffer from lack of food. They are simply doomed to a slow death." He then proposed that the entire Polish Army and all men fit for service be moved to Iran, where promised British aid in food and uniforms could be received and distributed. A well-outfitted and healthy army could then return to Russia to take up its own sector at the front.

General Panfilov was called in, and Anders complained that rations had been reduced from 44,000 to 30,000, and that on September 1 the entire army at Totskoie was without rations. Stalin reprimanded Panfilov, stating that he had ordered the rations increased. At the end, it was promised that sufficient supplies would be forthcoming and that the Polish Army would be properly organized on Russian soil. At an evening dinner Stalin gave for the Polish delegation, Anders recorded that the Poles complained of Soviet reluctance to release other Polish citizens who had been recruited into the Red Army and labor battalions from territories occupied in 1939. Stalin replied, "What do you care about White Russians, Ukrainians and Jews? You want Poles, they are the best soldiers."

The Soviets would be happy to have a friendly Polish force to help them defeat the Germans and restore order in a liberated Poland, but officials suspected an independently organized and led army. And supplies of all kinds were in short supply in the Soviet Union.

Anders insisted that his army's withdrawal south to Iran was agreed to by the Soviets, and he cited a letter from Soviet General Georgi Zhukov to that effect. Nevertheless, the Anders Army did not return to Russia. Soviet and Polish Communist propaganda spread accusations that the Anders Army did not want to fight the Germans. That's what we heard in the Berling Army and afterward in Communist Poland. The Anders Army distinguished itself in the Italian campaign of 1944–45. Its most notable accomplishments were the capture of Monte Cassino, liberation of many areas on the Adriatic coast, and taking the city of Bologna. These successes clearly contradict the Communist propaganda.

On April 25, 1943, diplomatic relations between the Soviet Union and the Polish government in London were severed. The cause was the discovery by the Germans in the beginning of 1943 of thousands of murdered Polish officers in mass graveyards in Katyn, near the city of Smolensk. The Germans accused the Russians of perpetrating this crime, while the Soviets categorically denied it. For the Poles, this solved the mystery of the missing ten thousand officers captured by the Soviets in 1939. The Polish government wanted an International Red Cross committee to investigate. The Soviets interpreted this as the Poles siding with the Germans, and therefore considered Poland an unworthy ally.

I think those events were the main ingredients that negatively influenced my fate and that of many other Poles during the increasingly strained relations between the Polish government in exile and the Soviet authorities. First, the evacuation of the Anders Army in the summer of 1942 precluded those who wanted to join a Polish Army from reaching that goal. There was no longer any nearby Polish Army to join. Poles continued to be kept in labor camps, exiled to Siberia and other places, and enlisted into Working Battalions of the Red Army (like the GUAS), all under extremely harsh conditions. Stalin's assertion that Jews did not belong in the Polish Army, and the decision to confer Soviet citizenship on inhabitants of the Soviet-occupied Polish territories, also had a direct and negative effect, one that affected me personally. Despite formally being a Soviet citizen I was not given the right to serve in the regular Soviet army. Moreover, when in the fall of 1943 I had managed to enter the Red Army, I was sent to a coal mine in Siberia, where I faced death within a few months. This was a clear conflict: either I was a Soviet citizen or I was a foreigner but I could not logically be both at the same time. The severance of diplomatic relations with the Polish government in London removed any source of protection for Polish citizens in the USSR. The Soviets were now free to adopt any repression against us they chose.

However, by November 1943, when I was sent to Siberia, a new Polish Army under the supervision of Polish Communists had been organized. Its First Division battled side by side with the Red Army. So why wasn't I sent to the new Polish Army? The answer came from Stalin's statement that Jews did not belong in it. And that was the reason given by the lieutenant in the Kandalaki coal mine for not sending me with the group going back to join the new Polish Army under General Berling.

It was late November 1943. Despite all the obstacles, I had arrived at the place where the First Polish Corps of the Kosciuszko (or Berling) Army had been organized. The Second Dabrowski Division had just left to join the Red Army in fighting the Nazis. The First Kosciuszko Division participated in the battle near the town of Lenino, in Mogilev *oblast* (province). Preparations were under way to form the Third Romuald Traugutt Division, named after the leader of the January 1863 Polish uprising against tsarist Russia.

Recruits were arriving daily from all over the Soviet Union, some released from prisons, some from worksites, both forced and voluntary. A large group consisted of prisoners of war from the German army taken by the Soviets; these prisoners were mostly residents of Silesia, the southern region of Poland, whom the Nazis claimed as *volksdeutsche*, ethnically related to Germans. However, they considered themselves Silesians: not exactly Poles, but certainly not Germans. The Silesian Poles didn't want to fight on the German side and surrendered to the Russians as soon as an opportunity arrived. They were good, well-trained soldiers.

A large number of Jewish refugees who fled the German occupation zone to the Soviet zone were deported in 1940–41 to Siberia, the northeastern region of Russia, and other outlying regions of the Soviet Union. A sizable part of them was now joining the Kosciuszko Army. Another source of recruits was of Jews from the territories of Poland that the Soviets annexed after September 1939, Jews who were able to escape eastward in the first days of the German-Soviet war in 1941. The Kosciuszko Army welcomed Polish Jews into its ranks; hence, they constituted a significant part of the enlisted volunteers in that army. Native Russian and Ukrainian officers of the Red Army were transferred by Soviet authorities, also, to serve as instructors and commanders in the Polish Army. Some of these officers had Polish ancestry.

12
A Jew in the Polish Army

Before WWI Jews and Poles as well avoided enlistment into the tsar's army if they could, in part because it required twenty-five years of service. After Poland regained its independence in 1918, Jews were Polish citizens with equal rights and were eligible to serve in the Polish Army. A significant number of Jews still tried to avoid military service for religious reasons, as they do in Israel today. When I joined the Polish Army I had to overcome this prejudice that was a part of my heritage, but I believed that it was no longer appropriate given the present circumstances.

In the army I had to undergo a significant adjustment. For the first time in my life I had to live among Poles. It may seem strange, but in prewar Poland, with its widespread anti-Semitism, Jewish communities were quite isolated. Poles commonly used insulting and derogatory language toward Jews; there were frequent physical assaults on them that could turn into general pogroms (as in Przytyk in 1936). Whenever possible, most Jews tried to avoid Christian Poles, choosing instead to live in areas with Jewish majorities.

When I was still a child I saw serious attempts by the younger generation of Jews in Poland to get out from that isolation. Young as well as many older Jews dressed in modern garments and did not wear beards or cover their heads. The "modernization" was supposed to remove one of the "reasons" why anti-Semites didn't like the Jews, but it did not seem to have any positive effect.

Marshal Jozef Pilsudski, Poland's head of State, was able to check somewhat the deeply felt animosity toward the Jews. Together with the entire nation we mourned his death in May 1935. Every Jewish school child sang the mourning song *"To nie prawda, ze Ciebie juz niema"* (It is not true that you are no more) because we loved this benevolent ruler. The situation for Jews changed dramatically after the so-called colonels took power. The Polish prime minister Slawoj-Skladkowski called for a boycott of Jewish enterprises. Anti-Jewish riots and pogroms took place in the years 1935–38: June 1935 in Grodno; March 1936 in Przytyk; April 1938 in Wilno and Dabrowa Tarnowska. The frequency of assaults on Jews increased dramatically. Jewish students were ordered to occupy the last row of seating at Polish universities and were often beaten up.

In a pastoral letter in February 1936 the head of the Polish Catholic Church, August Cardinal Hlond, advocated discrimination against Jews. He encouraged Catholics to fence themselves off against the Jews harmful moral influence, to separate themselves from its anti-Christian culture, and to boycott the Jewish press. At this time Julian Tuwim was a leading Polish poet; Artur Rubinstein, a world famous pianist; and Grzegorz Fitelberg, the director of the Warsaw Philharmonic and the Symphony Orchestra of the Polish Radio, to mention just a few Jewish luminaries in Poland's cultural life.

Hence not only was the effort of the new generation of Jews to leave the ghetto unsuccessful, it was accompanied by the call of Christians to further isolate the Jews.

Now circumstances had me sharing living quarters with Poles and, more importantly, relying on goodwill in situations that required comradeship and even personal sacrifice. There were also cultural adjustments to be made. Every morning and evening at roll call, we would sing the *Rota* (a patriotic song with anti-German and religious overtones) and *Boze Cos Polske* or *Kiedy Ranne Wstaja Zorze* (strictly religious songs with words like "God that bestows favor and protection on Poland"). It is significant that these songs were chosen, despite the highly visible influence of Communism on the political orientation of the army. These were, however, traditional Polish Army songs, and the leadership wanted to emphasize that we were a Polish Army.

I had a bit of a language problem as well. Before the war my spoken Polish skills were good, although at home we usually spoke Yiddish. I had attended an elementary school where by law instruction was in Polish. Having used Russian most frequently during the past three years, my Polish had become a little rusty. But I overcame this easily within a few weeks.

General Stanislaw Galicki, commander of my division, was the grandson of a participant in the 1863 Polish uprising against tsarist Russia, and who was then banished to Siberia. Romuald Traugutt, after whom our division was named, was the leader of that rebellion and was sentenced to death by the Russians. Galicki had been transferred from the Soviet army, and it certainly was an appropriate assignment. His Polish proficiency was initially not very good, although he worked hard to improve it. Many other Soviet officers were transferred into the Kosciuszko Army without a Polish background, and some could hardly speak the language even at the end of the war.

The atmosphere in the army was very good. I never observed or heard of anti-Semitic incidents of any kind. We all concentrated on training and preparing for the battles ahead. The officer corps insisted on camaraderie and cooperation among and within all units. The army and the country we were going to fight for were to be democratic, and therefore ideals of brotherhood and equality were guiding principles. The Communists who joined the army, among them many Polish Communists of Jewish origin, propagated these ideals. The deputy commander of the Third Division was Lieutenant Edward Ochab, who later became the first secretary of the Polish Workers Party and subsequently president of Poland. In 1968, at a critical time in Poland's history, he vigorously rejected the anti-Semitism adopted by the party leadership.

After a brief medical quarantine designed to prevent the spread of communicable diseases, I reported to the commander of the Eighth Regiment of the Third Division. The interview was brief. Colonel Karasiewicz looked at me and said, "We're sending you to noncommissioned officer's school." I responded, "*Tak jest obywatelu Pulkowniku*" (Yes, Citizen Colonel), and that was it. My experience in the Soviet army was doubtless certainly a factor in this selection.

I didn't have any problems with the training, although I can't say I enjoyed it. I liked the lectures of Lieutenant Michal Jekiel, chief instructor for the regiment. He looked like a general, and if I had had the power I would have bestowed that rank on him. He was my idol. At the end of the war Michal Jekiel was the deputy commander of our Third Division. After the war, with the rank of colonel, he was made the head of a state agency sponsoring sport and physical health.

After graduating on March 1944 from the ten-week course for non-coms, I was awarded the rank of corporal and appointed deputy leader of the First Platoon of the Seventh Company. The officer corps, including NCOs, stayed busy for the next few weeks training recruits (some of them more than fifty years old) who had arrived from all corners of the Soviet Union. By late

March 1944, the Third Division was ready to take the oath. A few weeks of preparation, mainly marching in parade formation, preceded the actual ceremony. The first date scheduled was canceled after several German planes were spotted cruising near the field where the division was to assemble. On March 26, 1944, on the second attempt, the division was sworn in. I remember clearly the command of the chief of staff of the division, Colonel Zajkowski: "*Dyvizjo sluszaj moju comandu!*" (Division, hear my command!), which was perfect Russian, not Polish. On the command "To the oath," everyone repeated solemnly: "I swear to the bleeding Polish land, and to the Polish nation under the tortured yoke, that I will not defile the name of a Pole and that I will faithfully serve my Fatherland." We swore to fight together with the Red Army, and we swore allegiance to the division's flag and to its motto, *Za Nasza i Wasza Wolnosc* (For our freedom and yours). After the oath, the division paraded in front of its commanders, foreign dignitaries, and guests.

I don't remember whether it was on that or some other occasion that I saw General Berling, our army's commander-in-chief, for the first time. He was a very tall man, a fitting figure for a general, very handsome and bold. He walked along addressing a crowd of soldiers and officers, and his shepherd dog followed the whole time. Before WWII, General Berling served in the Polish Army (*Wojsko Polskie*), reaching the rank of colonel, but was deactivated in 1939. After the Soviets occupied Wilno in 1939 he was imprisoned in Starobielsk with about eight thousand other Polish officers, most of whom disappeared in 1940. He joined the Anders Army but refused to leave the Soviet Union when that army was evacuated to the Middle East.

In January 1944 the Soviets liberated the long-besieged city of Leningrad and made some headway in the central part of Soviet territories occupied by the Germans. At the beginning of March 1944 for the first time in the Soviet-German war, the Soviet army began a spring offensive to follow the meager results of the winter offensive. The Soviets mounted two heavy thrusts, spearheaded by three tank armies. The Germans could not withstand the advancing force and so retreated. The Germans had been retreating since their defeat in the huge tank battle in the Kursk-Orel region in the summer of 1943. As a result of the spring offensive of 1944, the First Ukrainian Front commanded by Marshal Zhukov and the Second Ukrainian Front under the command of Marshal Konev reached the southwestern Pripet marshes, the foothills of the Carpathian Mountains and the lower River Dniestr, thereby liberating a significant part of the southeastern territories of prewar Poland by the middle of April. We realized that soon our army would join the fight to liberate our country.

In the spring of 1944 we trained on loading and unloading our gear, equipment, and personnel in and out of cattle cars. Everything had to be performed very fast since the railroad system was short of rolling stock and faced the need to deliver equipment, ammunition, and personnel for the next phase of the offensive. We repeated this exercise twice to make sure it would be perfect when the time came for the real movement. Loading the horses, our primary means of transportation, was the most difficult part. Our regiment was issued several hundred Mongolian horses that were extremely wild; they had roamed the steppes and had never been harnessed. These were much smaller than the horses we were used to dealing with in Europe, although much stronger. In the most demanding circumstances, the Mongolians performed better than other horses: they were to be of enormous help in the war, but initially did not easily submit to human will. Many soldiers who in civilian life were experienced handlers of horses tried to harness them, but it took several weeks to make the Mongolians obey.

On April 1 the railroad cars for our movement arrived at Rybnoye, a few miles from the city of Riazan. Finally we embarked for Poland to take part in the struggle for freedom. Our route went through the cities of Riazan, Kursk, Belgorod, Kharkov, Poltava, and Kiev, toward Rowne and the little train station of Kiwerce; a distance of about one thousand miles and a journey lasting almost six weeks. We stopped on the way several times, during which we trained intensively. Heavy bombardment by Germans occurred in Darnica, near Kiev. On the way we could see the terrible destruction in Kharkov as well as in many smaller towns and villages. We surmised that the Germans were applying a scorched-earth policy, and it was easy to imagine that we would find similar devastation in our country. We did not yet know much about the treatment of the Russian and Ukrainian population in the area. We knew even less about the plight of Jews. We were completely isolated from civilians. Either we were in the train or in large fields and forests, where the huge army could temporarily deploy and exercise. We received only official propaganda that the political apparatus deemed proper for us to know. I do not recall any reports at that time of the Nazi murderous program aimed at the Jewish people. The general tenor of the propaganda was that our army was going to liberate Poland, not specifically the Jews. However, from everything I had seen before I fled Poland, and from stories that filtered through the official news, I deduced that the Nazis were especially harsh toward the Jewish population. Yet no one in his sane mind could have imagined the magnitude of the genocide committed by the Nazis.

In addition to the hardships of travel in overcrowded and unsanitary cattle cars, our food supply was meager. The area we were now traveling through had been devastated by the war. Before retreating, the Germans managed to empty most of the warehouses. The newly reestablished Soviet authorities were not able to supply us with food.

On May 8, 1944, we arrived at the small station in Kiwerce, between the cities of Luck and Kovel. After marching the whole night, we reached the village Zofiowka and the nearby forest, where our regiment pitched camp. We were about thirty miles from the front lines and forty-five miles from the Bug River, the newly designated border between the Soviet Union and Poland. This frontier incorporated a large part of prewar Poland into the Soviet Union. We had known for some time about this change, which the authorities tried to justify by pointing out that Poland would regain its historical right to German territories in the west. Another reason cited was that in the territories annexed by the USSR, the population was mainly Ukrainian or Belorussian, and they should be united with their brethren in adjacent Soviet republics. This was a very controversial matter, but for us it was secondary to our coming struggle against the Nazis.

We expected that we would soon join the Soviet army in the fight against the Germans, but we still had to wait another two months during which we went through further training, including firing live ammunition. It looked like the Soviet command had decided to deploy the Polish Army in the liberation of Poland starting at the new frontier.

The Kosciuszko Army was now over 100,000 strong, complemented by Poles from the newly liberated Wilno area and other parts of eastern Poland. It was now the size of a full army and it was renamed the First Polish Army (1 *Armia Wojska Polskiego*), but I will continue to refer to it as I thought of it, as the Kosciuszko Army. Most of its force, except the First Division, had not engaged in battle during the more than six months since its formation. This was a departure from Soviet insistence that the Anders Army be deployed within a few short months from its formation.

13
The Kosciuszko Army Joins the Struggle

Finally the day arrived for us to leave. It was July 15, 1944, a symbolic date commemorating Poland's victory over the Germans at Grunewald (Tannenberg) on the same date in 1442. We burned our makeshift bunkers where we had camped for two months, since we did not want to leave the camp for use by unfriendly partisan groups operating in that area. The euphoria was high. I had waited for this moment for a long time, as had all the soldiers of our army. We knew we were entering into a struggle that would lead to the liberation of our country. I recall Colonel Jekiel on the day when we finally marched out from our temporary base in Sielce. He was mounted on a beautiful horse, and from the top of that majestic animal he congratulated me for being promoted to the rank of *plutonowy*, the equivalent of a sergeant. I felt that there was a reciprocal exchange of good feelings between us.

By that time the Soviet army launched its summer offensive. The First Belorussian Front was moving toward Warsaw. To its southern flank, the First Ukrainian Front was advancing to the city of Lwow. German resistance was weakened considerably by Hitler's decision to send a significant force to oppose the Western allied army that had already landed in Normandy. The Polish Army was now part of the Soviet offensive. On July 6, the left flank of the First Belorussian Front liberated the city of Kovel. The next task was to burst through German defenses on the Bug River and in coordination with the First Ukrainian Front, reach the Vistula River. The First Polish Army was assigned to participate in that offensive.

Each day brought us closer to the real action. Nobody actually told us what was going on. As we came closer, we didn't have to be told; we heard it. One could not clearly distinguish particular explosions but instead heard a general, almost uninterrupted roar. At that juncture I had ambivalent feelings, between the excitement of achieving my long-held goal of participation in the liberation of my country on one hand, and shock at the apocalyptic and fearsome reality beating against my ears on the other. From afar that roar seemed to me to be a wall of artillery spreading a deadly fire that no living creature could withstand. I was not sure whose artillery was so active and therefore didn't know what awaited us as we came closer with each day and hour of marching. As we approached the action, we could hear the explosion of individual artillery shells more clearly. We understood that as we got closer to the storm, we would have to plunge into the middle of it—and if the enemy were sending these fireballs, they would cause havoc among us. The first feelings of entering a big battle, despite our understanding that we were on the offensive, were not only joy and confidence. A soldier who had never gone through real fire has an exaggerated imagination that is very difficult to overcome. He thinks of it as hell, which it really is, and knows that he must enter it willingly, expecting the worst. That's how it was in my case. Thinking of the cataclysm that I was about to enter was very scary, since I supposed that even if it were our artillery that was so active, sooner or later, the Germans could respond in kind.

But they didn't! After eight days of advancing, we came close to the Bug River, the new frontier of Poland. Although it might seem routine for infantry units to cover long distances on foot, in this case it turned out to be very difficult. First of all, we always moved at night. Second, the terrain was sandy, and often our path led through forests. Above all, our infantry was not yet used to prolonged marches. Our shoes and the cloths wrapped around the feet instead of proper socks were not very suitable for long marches. Later in the war we learned how to avoid the many blisters and sometimes serious foot injuries. If one does not count those nightly marches with all our gear on our shoulders, from a strictly military point of view we were rather disappointed since so far our army's participation in that offensive was not significant. The Soviet army did most, if not all, the fighting. It seemed to me that the Soviet command did not consider the Polish Army well prepared enough to join a fast-moving offensive. On our march we were met by Soviet tank units returning from the front line, and they kidded the infantry for our slowness. We thought that we were doing our best. Yet I was certain that the Soviet commander was directing the Polish Army's movement, so we could enter the new Soviet-Polish frontiers as Poland's liberators.

This is how it happened: late in the evening of July 23 we reached a rather narrow crossing on the Bug River. There, a hastily erected bridge marked the point where we, the Polish Army, were going to enter the new Poland. After crossing the bridge, Polish and Soviet military and political officials greeted the heroic Polish Army, which was about to enter the final stage of liberating Poland. The next day, after a brief rest, we continued our movement forward, not meeting any resistance. The Germans were on the run, having decided to organize their defense on the Vistula River, closer to Warsaw. Good for us liberators! Our morale was high. We were excited, and it was so easy—but not for long!

In the meantime, we enjoyed tremendously the enthusiastic and, at times, suspicious greetings from the liberated Polish population. Since I was a deputy platoon commander, temporarily acting as deputy company commander, I often moved ahead of our main column. That gave me the opportunity to be among the first liberators of some villages and towns. Quite often we had to convince the peasants who greeted us that we really were a Polish Army. We had to speak in Polish, which was not a problem for most of us. Many times we had to point to the eagles on our hats to assure them that we were not the Red Army. However, our eagle was not precisely the one they remembered from prewar times. Ours was an eagle without the crown on his head that the prewar eagle had. After a time we were able to convince the liberated Poles that we were a Polish Army.

These were very brief encounters with liberated Poles, as we had to keep moving. They did not volunteer any information on what had happened to Jews. From my own experience and the letters from home received up to June 1941 I could infer that under Hitler Jews were terribly mistreated. I did not yet know of the atrocities the Nazis committed on the Jews of Europe, and the infrequent bulletins of the political department of the army did not report on this. Also, I think that the leadership of the Kosciuszko Army did not want to appear as Communist, Russian or Jewish, but as purely Polish in character. That attitude, even if it was not openly expressed, percolated into its person-nel by stressing its goal of liberating the Polish nation. Subconsciously I con-formed.

For the next five days, we continued toward Warsaw. The terrain approach-ing the city from the east was very sandy. Marching along narrow forest paths was extremely difficult. Often we followed artillery units, which cut very deep ruts. Even the carts carrying supplies or our mobile kitchens could carve deep tracks, which made it difficult for the infantry to follow. But we endured, keeping in the front of our minds that we were going to liberate Warsaw.

On several occasions the division commander, General Galicki, and Colonel Karasiewicz, the regimental commander, met us early in the morning after a very tiring march, bringing with them the division orchestra to lift our spirits. It worked well. I was additionally pleased because I could see my friend from the train escape from Siberia, the man who taught me to pilfer food from the other travelers. Now he was playing in the orchestra. He had a smile whenever he noticed me.

At the end of a full night's marching, some extremely tired and footsore soldiers would straggle from the main columns. Even the division orchestra playing quick-step *allegro molto vivace* marches did not help. Commanders at all levels, but especially the platoon and squad level, tried hard to encourage the stragglers to summon their strength to keep up with the main column. In some cases such soldiers would get a lift from the carts following us. Nevertheless, almost daily some soldiers would fall behind. I experienced for myself just how difficult it was to catch up with the main force.

One day the night march extended into the late morning hours. The regiment had to reach a rest area in a forest about three miles ahead. I could not keep up with the main column, and an increasing distance separated me from my unit. No military carts were behind me. The warming sun made my head spin, and my feet mistakenly assumed that it was time to rest. Initially a squad leader walked with me, but we were unable to close the distance to the main column. I was left alone. The area was safe, since it was probably liberated just the previous day. I applied all my will to continue walking. However, another internal power was holding me back, insisting on sitting down for a while. As the rests got longer it became more difficult to get up and walk. After a series of alternating rests and slow-motion walks lasting more than three hours, I finally reached my platoon. I made a very determined resolution never to allow myself another such experience.

I recall a tragic episode on another day of our offensive toward Warsaw. My favorite comrade was a tall man about fifty years old, a very good storyteller, full of common sense with a very pleasant and friendly manner. At the end of a night march we entered a little forest clearing, where we were supposed to rest during the day. As soon as we got the command to fall out, a number of soldiers moved some yards to the right, toward a river (the Vistula, I think). Suddenly several bombs fell on them. Within seconds I saw my friend's leg lying burned, and parts of his body spread all over the place, as were the bodies of several others. I was deeply saddened. The shock was so great not only because he was such a good friend, but also because he and the others were the first casualties that I experienced so closely. Later we got used to such events, considering them an inevitable consequence of the struggle for freedom. Nevertheless, it was as cruel later as it was then. Since it was so natural to turn toward the river, and for the first time I thought, "It could have been me."

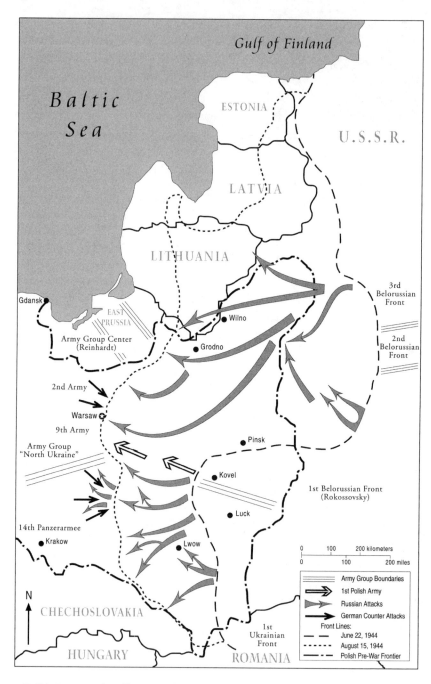

Gulf of Finland

Baltic
Sea

ESTONIA

U.S.S.R.

LATVIA

LITHUANIA

3rd
Belorussian
Front

Gdansk

EAST
PRUSSIA

Wilno

2nd
Belorussian
Front

Army Group Center
(Reinhardt)

Grodno

2nd Army

Warsaw

9th Army

Army Group
"North Ukraine"

Pinsk

Kovel

1st Belorussian Front
(Rokossovsky)

Luck

14th Panzerarmee

Krakow

Lwow

0   100   200 kilometers

0   100   200 miles

Army Group Boundaries

1st Polish Army

Russian Attacks

German Counter Attacks

Front Lines:

— — —   June 22, 1944

· · · · · ·   August 15, 1944

—·—·—   Polish Pre-War Frontier

N

CHECHOSLOVAKIA

HUNGARY

1st
Ukrainian
Front

ROMANIA

4. Polish Army on the offensive with the First Belorussian Front, 1944

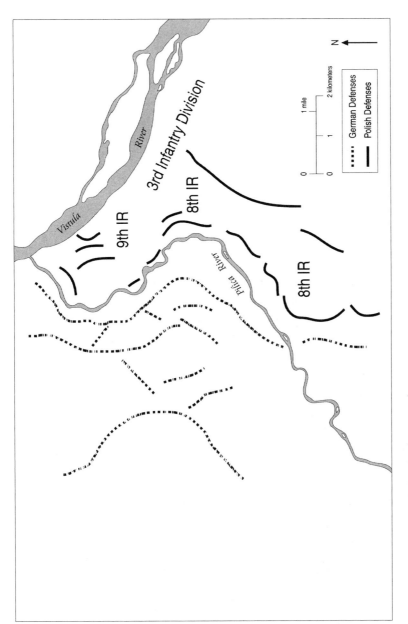

5. On the Magnuszew Bridgehead, July–September 1944

14
The Magnuszew Bridgehead

On the way to liberate Warsaw, we had to overcome significant resistance and suffer thousands of casualties. Our real first meeting with the enemy was in the area of the Pilica River (part of the Magnuszew Bridgehead called *Przyczulek Warecko-Magnuszewski*), approximately forty miles southwest of Warsaw. Before reaching that point, the First Polish Army was assigned to operate in the first line of the offensive of the First Belorussian Front between the cities of Deblin and Pulawy. The Polish divisions started fording the Vistula River from the right bank on the night of August 1, 1944. Its mission was to feign an attack on a relatively wide area, thereby diverting German attention from Soviet army operations further south, where an attempt was made to establish a bridgehead on the left bank of the Vistula. Two Polish divisions crossed the Vistula, but could not hold on. My Third Division was operating in the second line as a reserve. The Soviet operation was successful. The bridgehead on the left bank of the Vistula River, established by the Soviets under the command of General Vasily Ivanovich Chuikov, was twenty miles long and ten miles wide from the Pilica River on the north to the Radomka River on the south. At that time in the summer offensive, the Magnuszew Bridgehead was the most southwestern point held by the Soviet-Polish armies. It could be considered part of an attempt to encircle the German forces defending Warsaw. At the same time, it created a barrier against German attack on the southeastern flank of the offensive. The Germans held their line of defense on the left bank of the Pilica River.

My regiment and other units of the Third Traugutt Division were charged with holding the bridgehead and preventing the Germans from taking it back and cutting the road to Warsaw. The Soviet army held the first line of defense in the area. We arrived at the place where our units were supposed to take up the second and third lines of defense, which, for precautionary reasons, was to have been done at night. The Germans were about two miles away, on the other side of the Pilica River. My platoon commander, Lieutenant Franciszek Matejko, received coordinates and started assigning places where each soldier should dig his trench. He did so in accordance with military practice: he measured precisely the distance between each trench and it took him considerable time to finish this "important" task. Finally, around 3:00 A.M., every soldier knew exactly where his position should be. We had small personal spades and by dawn we were able to dig very shallow pits. The commander shouted to us to stop digging and take cover immediately.

Luckily, we thought, the fields had been recently harvested and plenty of wheat sheaves were available. We put the sheaves on top of our little shallow trenches, where we were supposed to remain until the next night. Since we put the sheaves in the military spacing, which was different from the order the peasants used, German reconnaissance planes had a very easy task in spotting us. They didn't shower us with bombs; they threw a few to greet us. So much for the extra precaution of our platoon commander! Ironically, the Soviet army was not so meticulous in obeying military regulations. The same morning as we were sitting behind the sheaves, we saw two figures approaching us from behind, moving toward the front line. When they came closer, we were surprised to recognize two Soviet soldiers unwinding the wire for field telephones in full view of the enemy.

An even more striking difference between Soviet behavior and ours on the front line was revealed a few days later, when we moved to the first line of defense to release the Soviet Twenty-seventh Infantry Division. We moved into position at night. The Soviet division was supposed to turn over to us all the intelligence they had gathered from observations over the previous week. They did a good job on that. Each position we took over was manned during the first night by units of both the Polish and Soviet armies. They showed us exactly where the enemy had placed their heavy machine guns, artillery pieces, and command posts. The next night, while the Soviet and Polish units were still in the trenches, we were entirely responsible for defense. The Soviet soldiers felt relieved and free, which gave them time for a little foray into the German trenches. They went without firearms, only knives and hand grenades. Officially they went for a "tongue," a live prisoner who could provide information about enemy units, armaments, and plans. The real aim of the escapade was to get some good food and liquor, of which they knew the Germans had plenty.

The operation was conceived and executed brilliantly. A few of our positions knew of their foray in order to provide cover in case of emergency, but mainly to let them out and back quietly. A group of six or seven Soviet soldiers departed at about midnight. They knew exactly which bunker the officers occupied. There they expected to find plenty of the sought-after spoils and maybe also a sleeping officer who would know a lot. Next, they had to figure out where the guards were located and what their movements were. With that knowledge clearly in mind, the group had to approach the place quietly, jump into the bunker, some to grab the German, gag and hustle him out, while the others seized the food and liquor. If necessary, they could use silent means to remove any unforeseen danger and then retreat as fast as possible. The night I was there, it worked out without a hitch. I learned that was not the first such escapade by this unit. The next night they left, and, for the first time, we were confronting the enemy at a distance of 300 to 400 yards across the little Pilica River.

We held this line of defense for thirty-three days. During that time there were small-scale skirmishes here and there. The Germans could not throw us out of our positions, and we did not intend to undertake any serious offensive either. Nevertheless, there was action on both sides of the front line, mainly firing from position at targets of opportunity. The most difficult part was spending so many days in open trenches. Although it was summer, the weather at night was not always pleasant, especially when it rained. Water caused the sides of our trenches to break down, requiring frequent repair. All night we had to watch the darkness to prevent the enemy from approaching without warning. Firing from their or our side from time to time interrupted the quiet, monotonous stalemate. There were a few forays against the German positions carried out by neighboring units. After a month of such skirmishes in that area, the Soviet army replaced our unit.

During those thirty plus days I had plenty of time to think about what had happened to my parents and siblings. It had been more than three years since I had heard from them. On a dark night thoughts freely range to imagine the worst. I was sure that they were starving, that merely finding food required heroism against dangers greater than I faced in the front lines. I also feared that they were defenseless against Germans eager to shoot at will. So their situation was much worse than mine. I could without anybody's permission send a series of bullets from my automatic rifle toward the German trenches if I sensed danger. But even in the darkest corners of my mind I could not suspect that a terrible machine designed to murder had been set in motion to kill millions and that my loved ones could become or already had been its victims. If I had known this, sitting in those trenches and stretching my vision toward the nearby enemy, the war would have acquired a sharper, much more determined and personal meaning. Not knowing this then, the month I spent sitting in a trench seemed only a depressing hardship.

15
In Support of the Warsaw Uprising

While it was reasonably quiet at the Magnuszew Bridgehead, dramatic and politically charged events took place not far from it, in the Warsaw area. By the end of July 1944 broadcasts from Moscow were encouraging the people in Warsaw to rise against the Germans. On August 1, 1944, the Home Army (Armia Krajowa, AK), which reported to the Polish government in exile in London, began a general uprising in Poland's capital. The Soviet army, under the command of Marshal Konstanty Rokossovsky, had advanced toward Warsaw and reached its outlying suburbs by August first. Then the offensive came to a sudden halt.

What happened to stop that powerful Soviet advance that withdrew even from captured territory near Warsaw? Whether or not the military situation required it I am unable to judge. Many sources reported that Marshal Rokossovsky's offensive met unexpectedly strong resistance and counterattacks from several German Panzer divisions at the approaches to Warsaw. Other historians question that interpretation of events, ascribing political motives to the sudden halt of Marshal Rokossovsky's offensive at Praga, a suburb of Warsaw. Marshals Rokossovsky and Zhukov submitted a plan to Stalin that would have renewed the offensive on August 8, 1944. However, that plan was ignored and a limited advance to take Praga did not begin until September 10.

Events surrounding the Warsaw Uprising had a profound effect on the Polish capital, its population, and the unit of the Kosciuszko Army in which I served. For many reasons, it was the most emotional episode of my war with the Nazis. For one we were psychologically programmed to assume that taking Warsaw was our main goal in the war. Second, it was close to the city of

Lodz where I was born and where I lived, and I was anxious to liberate my hometown. Had we taken Warsaw at that time I would have been only a few days away from Lodz. Third, I still held in my memory the beauty of Warsaw that I saw in 1939 on my way to the Soviet-occupied territories of Poland. Finally and very important, many of my comrades lost their lives for a purely political strategy unworthy of their sacrifice.

Before deciding to authorize the Warsaw Uprising, the Polish government in London reached a critical moment in its existence. The Home Army loyal to the Polish government in London fought the Germans by direct battle with German units, through sabotage missions, and by assembling intelligence used by the allied forces. It changed tactics when Soviet armies were about to enter prewar Polish territories. The AK began to attack the rearguards of retreating Germans, thereby cooperating tactically with the Soviet forces. When the Soviets entered prewar Polish territories, the Home Army units were supposed to emerge from hiding and undertake administration of the liberated areas. This strategy, called *Burza* (Tempest), was applied in Volhynia and in the two biggest cities east of the Curzon line (the new border between Poland and the Soviet Union favored by Stalin), Lwow and Wilno. The results were disastrous for the Home Army. After the Soviet army liberated those places, they arrested the leadership of the Home Army units and offered the rank-and-file soldiers a chance to join the Berling Army. Most of them rejected the offer and their AK units were dissolved. Those who expected that such treatment of an allied army would cause a strong reaction from the western allies were disappointed. Neither Great Britain nor the United States was prepared to defend Poland's claim to its prewar eastern territories. Stalin, Churchill, and Roosevelt confirmed this at the Teheran conference in November 1943.

In the meantime, combat units of the Communist *Armia Ludowa* (People's Army) became active in 1943, especially as the Soviet army approached the Bug River. The majority of Polish people under German occupation were resigned to the fact that only the arrival of the Soviet army could bring liberation. The AK and other small units of underground fighters could not by themselves defeat the German occupiers. They could play only an auxiliary role, which was exactly how the AK command saw its opportunity to assist in the defeat of the Germans, and expressed in the "Tempest" strategy.

In the spring of 1944 underground leaders of the AK were fully aware that they were losing ground to their Communist rivals. They were also not at all certain what the Polish people's response to the Red Army would be. Large sections of the people, desiring speedy deliverance from the German yoke above all, were ready to hail the Soviet army as their liberators. In November 1943 Tadeusz Bor-Komorowski, commander of the AK, admitted that: "Among the masses a tendency to regard the Soviets as their rescuers from the German terror has begun to emerge." This view was prevalent in the summer of 1944. The leadership of AK, keenly aware that many Poles were vulnerable to Communist political propaganda, urged the government in London to respond with promises of political and social reform to offset the Communist appeal. That request signified that the Polish exile government in London was losing ground in the political arena as well. Finally, the Soviet-supported administration in the liberated parts of Poland (PKWN, the Polish Committee of National Liberation) took hold. Under those circumstances the London government decided to play its last card: create a *fait accompli* in Warsaw by starting the insurrection with the hope of establishing its administration in the capital.

At the start of the Warsaw Uprising, Stanislaw Mikolajczyk, the prime minister of the London government, was in Moscow. At a meeting with Soviet foreign minister Molotov, Mikolajczyk announced that he had given approval for an uprising to assist the advancing Soviet army. Molotov was not impressed. In a subsequent meeting on August 3, 1944, Mikolajczyk tried to convince Stalin to assist the Warsaw Uprising. However, Stalin considered the uprising an unfriendly act designed to prevent the authorities established in Lublin, dominated by Polish Communists and supported by the Soviets, from assuming the leadership of postwar Poland.

In the meantime, the poorly armed Home Army was losing ground in the city and, except for a few initial successes, was driven out from most positions and systematically slaughtered. The Germans decided to completely destroy Poland's capital. They systematically incinerated the city; for weeks flames could be seen from many miles away. This was what we saw when our Polish units approached the eastern suburbs of Warsaw.

Great Britain and the United States tried to support the uprising by sending planes from bases in Italy to airlift arms and food supplies. The Western powers repeatedly asked the Soviets to let their planes use Russian airfields to refuel on their way back from missions to Warsaw. Stalin rejected such requests several times. The ministers of the British war cabinet sent a direct letter to Stalin, expressing concern over the policy, which they regarded as at variance with the spirit of the anti-German alliance. Churchill even considered halting the supply convoys to the USSR in retaliation, but was persuaded not to by his Foreign Office. Roosevelt hardly shared the outrage of the British, and on September 5, 1944, sent a curious telegram to the British leader in which he cited information supposedly supplied by American intelligence, that the insurgents had left Warsaw and the problem had therefore solved itself.

On September 13, 1944, our Eighth Regiment of the Berling Army left the Magnuszew Bridgehead and, together with the entire Third Division was ordered to Praga, the eastern suburb of Warsaw. The Soviet army started its assault on Praga on September 10, with the First Kosciuszko Division of the Polish Army taking part in the offensive. On September 15 the Eighth Regiment reached Praga and started preparing to provide help to the insurgents in Warsaw. General Berling, commander of the First Polish Army, gave orders to the Third and Second Divisions to cross the Vistula into downtown Warsaw in support of the insurrection. The Eighth Regiment was then in Grochow, another suburb of Warsaw, about three miles from the Vistula. We were spread out in private houses, with the civilian population that had remained or followed the Soviet army back into the town. These people received the Polish Army with exceptional warmth. The spirit of the civilians was very high. I do not recall any bitterness over their situation under German occupation just a few days before. All their concern was over what was happening in the burning city of Warsaw across the Vistula. No wonder, as apart from their deep patriotic feelings most of them had relatives, friends, and fellow fighters engaged in a mortal struggle with the hated Nazis.

The Poniatowski Bridge on the Vistula, although partly destroyed, was now within walking distance. I crossed that bridge in 1939 on my way to the Soviet-occupied territories of Poland. Now my division had the task of taking that bridge back from the Nazis and liberating Warsaw. I was very excited by that prospect. Up to now I was involved in the liberation of places not familiar to me. But the Poniatowski Bridge across the Vistula was still in my mind, as if I had crossed it only the day before. I remembered my excitement on that November 1939 morning at the sight of such a large river with its glittering water and its majestic bridge. In 1939 those feelings were mixed with fear, as I was apprehensive over a possible meeting with a German soldier. Those feelings were also mixed with the hope that soon I would be free of such fear. Now in 1944, the prospect was to liberate the bridge and cross that river. I felt that I was about to take back a piece of land that had once been mine, even though I had crossed the bridge only once in my life.

After a short preparation, we embarked on the approach toward Warsaw. The enthusiastic population wished us success in liberating the capital and accompanied us for about a mile or two. The girls near the columns of marching soldiers were dressed in their best clothes as if going to a holiday party. They were excited and agitated. No wonder, as some of them were seeing a Polish army for the first time, and other, older ones after five dark years of German occupation. I am sure they believed we would liberate Warsaw by joining the fighters on the other side of the Vistula. Our feelings easily matched theirs, since we were on our way to take Warsaw!

As we came closer to the bridge, we asked the civilians to return to their homes since we were entering a very dangerous zone, where hostile fire could cause many casualties. We turned left toward Saska Kepa, a beautiful suburb on the right bank of the Vistula, and heavy artillery fire greeted us almost immediately at our arrival. Artillery shells were exploding around us, hitting buildings and advancing units alike. A few enemy planes tried to penetrate to our side of the river, but were shot down as soon as they showed up on the horizon. Despite the heavy enemy fire, our casualties were not high, since we could take cover in the buildings. Nevertheless, the commander decided to withdraw his units, considering further advance under such conditions too costly. We got orders to abandon the attempt to ford the river and return to our quarters in Grochow. We were disappointed and somewhat dispirited. However, we were certain that we would try again.

The more I think about that operation, the more I wonder about the orders we received. How could we ford the river without any equipment? We had only our regular weapons with us, nothing more. Maybe some engineer units were preparing means for crossing the river, but I did not know of any.

The next day we set out again for another try. My unit advanced to the right of the Poniatowski Bridge into an undeveloped field near the Kierbedzia Bridge, where the Stadion Dziesieciolecia sports arena now stands. We were easily detected by the Germans and were met by a furious barrage of artillery fire that we could not withstand. We retreated quickly, running through the field to get out of the fire zone. There were casualties.

I had my doubts about this operation immediately and for many years thereafter. It was not clear to me why we approached those positions in daylight in highly visible columns marching as if we were in a parade. Were our commanders that inept?

While we remained in Grochow near Plac Szembeka, I saw large squads of Western allied bombers flying across the frontline with impunity. I did not hear any explosions caused by those aircraft. According to Western sources, on September 18, 107 American bombers from bases in Britain, flew to Warsaw, dropped their supplies to the insurgents in the city, and flew on to the Soviet airbase in Poltava with Stalin's knowledge and consent. The historian Martin Gilbert states: "Of the 1,284 containers of arms and supplies dropped, about 1,000 fell into German hands. In all, 306 allied aircraft had flown over Warsaw, with Polish, British, American and South African crews; 41 were shot down, and at least 200 airmen killed."

On the same day, September 18, from Plac Szembeka for the first time I saw the firing of the powerful *Katiusha* artillery. That was the only Soviet artillery support that I observed at the time. It is possible that there were other instances, but not during our attempts to cross the Vistula. The *Katiusha* was the Soviets' most powerful artillery piece, and was not yet entrusted to the friendly Polish Army. The area on Plac Szembeka was cleared within a radius of about two hundred yards. The roar as the *Katiusha* simultaneously released sixteen shells was deafening. No wonder the Germans feared them. The shelling was directed at Warsaw or its outlying suburbs.

Our next attempt was carried out at night. We reached the Vistula and began to cross with the objective of landing in downtown Warsaw on the far side. The Ninth and Seventh Regiments of the Third Division got orders to cross the Vistula on September 19, 1944. They started under a smoke screen spread over a wide area. The Eighth Regiment was operating as a reserve in the second echelon. Later that night almost all companies of our Eighth Regiment got into boats with as many light arms as possible, under orders to reach the left bank of the river. The smoke screen was supposed to hide the advancing units from the enemy. I am not sure that such a smoke screen was helpful even though it covered a wide area. I am inclined to think it rather indicated where the floating units were. The Germans on the other side of the river directed their fire at the smoke, hitting our loaded boats. For several hours of this operation I witnessed relentless artillery fire at our units. Although I could not see individuals flung into the air when a German shell hit a boat, I did see the explosions and the erupting balls of fire. I saw so many of these

I could easily imagine the magnitude of the disaster. After a while my Seventh Company was supposed to embark. I thought that this was probably the end, as it was for most of the soldiers on the river.

As far as I know no Soviet or Polish artillery or air units were supporting the advancing units. I did not hear nor witness any, at least not in the area I was in. There must have been a good reason for this. After all, we were trying to reach the combatants fighting in the uprising on the left bank of the river, where they were supposed to hold their positions. Our artillery could not direct its fire at their positions nor at the city still inhabited by more than a million people. Nevertheless, artillery and air support could have been directed at the German positions in and around the city, thus assisting the uprising indirectly and providing cover for us.

The army units that managed to reach the left bank of the river had to fight Germans instead of being met by friendly forces. The whole operation, both on the river and on its left bank, was a colossal fiasco. Most of the units that reached the other side were destroyed. Only a few soldiers managed to retreat to areas between the bridge columns where they hid. Others tried to swim back across during the next few nights. According to official accounts, 485 soldiers from our regiment were killed in that operation. Other units of the Third and Second Infantry Divisions suffered many more casualties.

There are many ways one can survive the horrors of war. Most are due to a lucky confluence of circumstances. In this instance, I was lucky again. My Seventh Company of the full Eighth Regiment (there are nine companies and several special units in an infantry regiment) was assigned to remain on the right bank to help load heavy artillery pieces onto boats, but that operation was called off before the artillery tried to cross the river.

Our last attempt to assist the Warsaw Uprising failed miserably. Warsaw was burning; the city was losing its struggle for liberation. This was the biggest failure of our army in the entire war.

Early the next morning after that failed operation, while I was still on the right bank, a group of high-ranking Soviet officers passed by. In an interview I gave in 1972 to Professor Zawodny I recalled, "Sometime around four or five o'clock in the morning, a group of high-ranking Russian officers, including generals, came into the area shouting, implying that we had created a mess, and asking where our commander was. They wanted to know why Poles had not told them that they were going to cross the river. The officers said that, had they known, they would have provided artillery and air assistance."

Zawodny then states: "The sergeant's impression was that this Polish action in crossing the river was without Soviet approval, and there is strong supporting evidence, for many commanders of units within the First Polish Army were removed from their positions by the Soviet command after this action, among them General Galicki, commander of the 3rd Division, and General Berling." The appearance of high-ranking Soviet officers and their expressions of surprise led me to believe then that the operation was not approved by the Soviet command. Berling disappeared for the remainder of the war, only to reappear in 1947 as the chief of the Scientific Institute of the Polish Army.

However, on further reflection, it seemed implausible that the Soviet command didn't know what was going on in such an important part of the front. Two Polish divisions approached the Vistula River several times and the front commander didn't know of it? I think that the Soviet officers staged a sideshow to deflect their responsibility for the failed operation.

The Agreement between the Soviet Government and the Polish Committee of National Liberation of July 27, 1944, states: "In all zones of operation of Soviet troops and Polish armed forces, the Polish forces will be under the Soviet Commander-in-Chief for operational matters . . . " It is inconceivable that Generals Berling and Galicki decided on their own to send two divisions of the Polish Army to cross the Vistula and help the Warsaw insurgents. The punishment for such insubordination would have been very severe, far worse than removal from command.

According to Norman Davis, author of *Rising '44*, "With Marshal Rokossovsky's assent, therefore, Gen. Berling issued an order on 16 September 1944. Units of the 1st Battalion, 9th Infantry Regiment of the First Polish Army were to force the Vistula and to link up with the insurgents." I agree with Davis that there was a clear understanding and agreement between the two Polish generals and Marshal Rokossovsky on the First Polish Army's role in the Warsaw Uprising. However, a few days after the Polish Army launched the mission, Stalin told American ambassador Averell Harriman that Berling's action in trying to make contact with the insurgents in Czerniakow was "against the better judgment of the Red Army." Could Marshal Rokossovsky have told the Polish generals "don't do it" and they didn't follow his advice? It is inconceivable.

The withdrawal of the Third Traugutt Division from the Magnuszew Bridgehead and its replacement by a Soviet Division could not have happened without the explicit order of Front Commander Marshal Rokossovsky. Moreover, the Polish division was not involved in the liberation of the Warsaw suburb Praga. Instead, it was charged with crossing the Vistula in support of the uprising. Can any serious analyst conclude that the Soviet marshal did not know about those movements? The answer is clear. Marshal Rokossovsky knew of and approved the whole operation.

My hypothesis that explains all these Machiavellian statements and actions is that Soviets and the Polish Communist authorities in Lublin were confronted with a serious political dilemma. Both were already sure that they would have to govern Poland after the victory over Germany, and both were sure that the majority of the population would be opposed to the Communist regime that they were about to install. The Soviets were already losing credibility by allowing the Warsaw Uprising to be crushed by the Germans. It was a moment that would be remembered. Had the Polish Army not tried to stretch out a hand to its brothers in Warsaw, it would have been seen as a puppet army to be hated as an enemy of the Polish nation. Aware of that problem, the commanders of the Polish Army came to an agreement with the Soviets to undertake a rescue mission across the Vistula River. But the Soviets were not interested in seeing the uprising succeed, as that would be to the advantage of the Polish government-in-exile. Thus Berling organized a mission bound to fail. The Polish authority could then boast that it was trying to help the insurrection organized by "the political bankrupts from London." The Polish Army, always admired by the nation, could thereby preserve prestige in the eyes of a majority of people, helping paving the way for the installation of a Soviet regime in Poland.

It is clear that the Soviets did not want the Home Army, connected to the Polish government-in-exile in London, to establish itself as a force in Warsaw with which the Soviets would have to deal. Stalin preferred that the uprising fail, no matter how much the city and its population would suffer as a result. That defeat had enormous consequences for the Warsaw population and the city itself. Several hundred thousand Warsaw inhabitants, not only insurgents, were killed or sent to concentration camps. The city was completely destroyed.

I elaborate so much on this war episode because it was the final attempt by the London-based government to make good on its claim of the right to govern Poland. Looked at from the other side, the defeat of the Warsaw Uprising was a victory for the nascent Communist system in Poland. That victory was achieved at the expense of the heroic insurgents of Warsaw, and of several hundred thousand inhabitants killed, and of the destruction of Poland's capital. I was physically and emotionally involved in that drama on the right bank of the Vistula River. I saw a part of the political game played by the Soviet government that was rarely witnessed by a low-ranking soldier. Even if I did not understand at that time how the game was being played, I saw the Soviet officers put up a smoke screen that was supposed to hide their true purpose. And I was emotionally shocked by the enormity of our casualties, surpassing our losses in all other operations.

I am frequently asked whether I felt fear during the war. I indicate a few places where this was the case. There were only a few because about 80 percent of my unit's operations were on the offensive, as we chased the retreating Germans. Then excitement and euphoria prevailed. In the operation across the Vistula, after witnessing the massacre of my regiment and as I was about to enter the boat, I had no fear. Something worse than fear took reign over me: resignation. I did not believe that there was a chance to get out of there alive. I had no choice, I had to go. Fear would have paralyzed me. Resignation made me free. Luckily I did not come to the final test.

After the Vistula disaster, we were withdrawn to little towns surrounding Warsaw on the east side of the river. Among other duties the Seventh Company was assigned to guard 10,000 tons of flour apparently sent by Stalin as a gift to the people of Warsaw. In the middle of a huge plaza in the town of Milosna, 100,000 sacks of flour were placed in a heap that measured about three hundred yards long, thirty yards wide, and three yards high. While we were there, no distribution of that gift took place.

A few weeks later, we returned to the river once more, this time in a defensive posture. Along the right bank of the Vistula north of Warsaw, the river bank was surmounted by a bulwark on which we arranged our defensive positions. We built bunkers, with observation and firing positions on top of the bulwark and trenches along its bottom. It was a dream position for defense. Elevated above the ground and protected by the river in front, we could sit there forever. Obviously, this was not our goal. We wanted to be there as short a time as possible and to resume our effort to liberate Warsaw. As it turned out, we spent more than two months there, and we even managed to have some fun.

While sitting in the makeshift observation points, we used newly acquired tracing bullets to shoot at enemy positions, and we watched the bullets bounce back into the air when they hit some hard object. But most of the fun focused on our ability to shoot Germans with relative impunity. My favorite game was to empty onto the top of the bulwark a kettle of porridge which we received daily as part of our food ration. Overnight, the porridge froze (it was now November and December, with below-freezing temperatures), and it looked to the Germans like a soldier's head. Their sharpshooters considered it an opportune target. We sat deep in our bunkers watching German tracers bounce back when they "hit the grits." It was not entirely a safe game, but it was fun and it reflected our seasoning as soldiers and our disregard for the enemy.

An even riskier, but more meaningful game was the 1945 New Year's Day celebration. At exactly midnight on December 31 we started a spectacle with all the fire power at our disposal. Heavy and light artillery, heavy and light machine guns, individual rifles, everything and everyone participated in more than an hour of firing, letting the Germans know that the New Year would be our year of victory and the end of the war. The Germans were hiding on their side of the river, probably surprised by our attack and wondering whether this was the beginning of the winter offensive, which they knew always came at this time of year. Not until about 3:00 A.M. did they decide to respond in kind, shooting toward our side. Luckily, we were dug in safely and did not suffer any casualties. But it was not always safe. Many times German artillery shelled at us. Since we had built a trench along and below the bulwark, it was easy to jump into the trench whenever the Germans started shooting. Yet a few times there were casualties.

Several attempts to capture prisoners were made by our reconnaissance units. In most cases, these were special units, trained to carry out such operations. But there were also penal companies, made up of soldiers punished for serious offenses. Those companies were usually given the most dangerous tasks.

In December, when the river started freezing, our platoon was ordered to go down the river to measure the thickness of the ice, for the commanders needed information about crossing conditions on the Vistula for the winter offensive. This was dangerous because of systematic German rocket fire to illuminate the area. They had the habit of firing those rockets to make sure that we didn't fall asleep during the night; more seriously, they were watching to see whether we were approaching in the darkness. Danger was also created by nature itself. We had to advance out into the river as far as possible and bring back pieces of ice that we cut out there. It was easy to step too far onto thin ice over the main channel, and when the ice broke, the soldier would have a really cold bath. The trick used to avoid such bad luck was to link everyone together with a strong rope and then approach the river in a line. If the ice broke under the feet of the soldier in front, those behind him would be able to pull him out. Such a reconnaissance was my first command of an entire group effort, and I was proud of it, knowing that the result of our mission would be submitted to regiment and division command.

It was a freezing, dark night. The Vistula bank on our side had a layer of thick shrubs. It was quiet, the air refreshingly chilly. We were concerned that we would be discovered by the Germans; as we pushed our way through the shrubs we made noise that we thought was echoed on the other side. We crouched down, waiting for an illuminating rocket to go off. After one did, we had an interval that we could exploit to move out onto the river. The closer we came to the middle of the Vistula, the riskier it was to be detected if we made too much noise. There we had to use axes to cut out pieces of ice. We held our breath, wielding the axes with utmost care so as not to attract German attention.

Having cut sufficient pieces of ice from different areas of the river, we started withdrawing. On our way back, another rocket flash lit the sky but we were already in the shrubs near our bank. The feeling of a successful mission relieved our tension. We delivered proof that the river was not yet frozen enough, and that the ice was still too thin to carry military personnel, much less heavy equipment. The time for our winter offensive had not yet arrived.

16
Liberating Warsaw

We remained in that defensive position on the Vistula riverbank until January 6, 1945. Commanders allowed us a few days of rest to prepare for the big battle for Warsaw. We didn't have to wait too long. On January 12, 1945, we headed south. We marched only at night, avoiding villages and contact with civilians. Orders were to proceed with extreme caution: no smoking, no campfires, and no loud talking. Our regiments moved along the Vistula River on its right bank, while the Germans observed everything from the other side. The Polish Army was now part of a huge offensive designed to finish the war. The January 1945 Soviet offensive is considered the largest military operation of World War II. The First Belorussian and First Ukrainian Fronts, both operating from the Vistula to the north and south of Warsaw, had 2.2 million troops against German Army Group A with about 400,000 men. After three days of advance, our regiment along with the entire Kosciuszko Army reached the area of concentration in the vicinity of Kolbiel. These marches were extremely difficult, since we could not enter any village to rest. The temperature was below freezing, at nights reaching 0°F.

On the night of January 17, the advance was extremely slow. The first units of our army approached the Vistula across from the west bank town of Gora Kalwaria, where we were to cross the river. The infantry had no problem crossing the thick ice. Our concern was for the artillery and other heavy equipment and supplies. Would the ice hold? In most instances, it did.

I do not recall any serious fighting as we crossed the frozen Vistula. Resistance had already been suppressed by artillery fire from the Soviet and Polish armies. The Germans were expecting the winter offensive, and they tried to withdraw while there was still an opportunity to do so. Several thrusts by the

Soviet army sought to encircle the Germans; hence, they desperately tried to get out as soon as possible.

Early in the morning of January 17, 1945, we reached the far side of the river, entering the town of Gora Kalwaria. I was ecstatic! We ran excitedly uphill from the river. There were no people around. The enemy must have left not long before, since many buildings were still smoldering. I knew Gora Kalwaria by name from before the war as the seat of the Gerrer Rebe, one of the famous rabbis of my time; the other was the Alexanderer Rebe, from Aleksandrow, a small town not far from Lodz. Both had an enormous following among Orthodox Jews. The two camps were in fierce competition, arguing whose rebbe was more learned, wiser, better at judging disputes, and giving advice—and, above all, the holiest. Although I was not a follower of either, I had great respect and admiration for both, and felt pride that I was now participating in the liberation of this famous place.

After several days of marching and the difficult night of January 17, we had hoped that we would be allowed some rest before moving forward again. However, orders were to push forward as fast as possible. We continued on all day and covered in one day a distance that took us several days to accomplish on the way south. The orders were to take Warsaw that same day: January 17. We passed through several Warsaw suburbs, such as Piaseczno, Pyry, and Sluzewiec, where the population greeted us enthusiastically. In addition to flowers and kisses, we were flooded with moonshine made from wheat, potatoes, sugar and, most frequently, beets. The latter didn't taste good, but we didn't mind. By late evening, we entered Mokotow, the southern district of Warsaw proper. It was an empty ghost city. When we reached the area assigned to our battalion it was already dark, so we couldn't get a close look at the devastation of the city. That would have tempered our euphoria over our reception in the suburbs. Nevertheless, it was not difficult to find nice empty apartments in the surviving buildings. For the first time in many months, we slept on soft mattresses in civilized conditions. Were the Germans sleeping on them the night before? Maybe! Even that added to the realization that we were the victors. Our dream to liberate our capital had come true.

17
Racing to Berlin

Many of our comrades naïvely thought that for us the war was now almost over. In fact we had to get up early the next morning and continue the offensive. So much for sleeping on good mattresses! On January 18, we marched down the main streets of Warsaw: Aleje Jerozolimskie and Marszalkowska. Sadly, these were no longer the beautiful avenues but, rather, narrow lanes cleared through piles of mortar, bricks, and other debris from destroyed buildings. Some areas had not yet been cleared of mines left by the enemy, and those who stepped outside the cleared pathways were endangering themselves and their comrades. There were some casualties.

The difference between the enthusiastic welcome we received in the Warsaw suburbs and the silence in the empty city of Warsaw was depressing. To say that Warsaw was a ghost city is not sufficient. From what we had seen on January 18, 1945, we had to conclude that the city was no more. As far as the eye could see were huge expanses of debris in the midst of which a ruined building occasionally could be seen. One could doubt if the city would be rebuilt and how long it would take. If there was any reason to hope, it was sparked by the Warsaw residents that we saw returning on the same day we were leaving the city. Women, some old, carrying bundles of meager belongings or pushing a wheelbarrow loaded with a few chairs or other items necessary to reestablish a semblance of living, streamed back into their beloved city. It was the middle of winter, but Warsawians did not want to wait for warmer weather. These examples of patriotism and love of Warsaw were indications of the enormous human resources that the city would mobilize in its resurrection.

Personally, I was not disappointed to continue advancing, since this brought me closer to my home, Lodz, which was only eighty miles southwest of Warsaw. I fervently hoped that I would find my family there and be able to provide some help. We made good progress in our advance during the day. The entire First Belorussian Front, including the First Polish Army, was pushing forward west of Warsaw. The next day we reached the city of Sochaczew, which indicated that we were heading northwest, away from the direction of Lodz, the city I longed to liberate. I was desperate, broken-hearted. We were so close, only some fifty miles from the place I had made my personal goal to return to as a liberator. And now the commander was taking it away from me, ordering a turn northward instead of to the south.

All these five long years I had hoped I would be able to liberate my family, to show my true feelings for them, not in words but in action. In my desperation I considered leaving my regiment and joining other units that were headed southwest. However, my comrades strongly advised me against any such desperate move, as it could be considered desertion. I couldn't act against military discipline; the consequences of such disobedience could be dire. Several times I had witnessed the punishment of Polish Army deserters by execution.

After so many years it is impossible to discern exactly when I learned of the nearly total annihilation of the Jews of Poland. In the Polish Army nothing was announced on that subject. While liberating the southeastern part of Poland I could have heard isolated stories of the executions of Jews; they certainly were told together with accounts of similar acts against the non-Jewish population. The army was moving fast, and the opportunity to mingle with civilians was extremely limited. I was not aware of the death camp in Majdanek, a suburb of Lublin, because my unit did not take part in its liberation. I learned about it later. Information about the outside world was very limited. No newspapers or radios were available. The army was isolated. This way the political leadership could convey to soldiers only that news that furthered their goals. Our first chance to speak extensively with civilians was in the eastern suburbs of Warsaw in September 1944. There I learned about the Jewish uprising in the Warsaw ghetto in the spring of 1943, but then our overwhelming concern was for the current uprising in Warsaw. Hence, I could still believe and hope that my family and relatives were still alive and that I had a chance to liberate them. This was my dream and I was so close to realizing it—I was only fifty miles from Lodz!

At Sochaczew we had a hard time crossing the Bzura River. The bridge was out, and Soviet and Polish units were trying to cross on very thin ice; crowds of soldiers, heavy equipment, carts, and even some light trucks moved forward in a mixture of Russian and Polish shouts of "faster, hurry up, push the artillery!" On a narrow path around the destroyed bridge hundreds of soldiers surged across the Bzura, attempting to assist artillery crews in pushing their cannons over the rough and broken ice. There were long delays, and more units of both armies were still arriving to add to the crowd on the ice.

Our next encounter with the enemy took place a few days later, near Bydgoszcz, a large and important city on the route north to the Baltic and southwestward to Berlin. The importance of liberating Bydgoszcz was evident from the large concentration of units of the Soviet and Polish armies. Soviet units reached the outskirts of the city on January 20, 1945. The Germans tried frantically to organize a defense of Bydgoszcz. At the same time, they destroyed anything useful to prevent them from falling into our hands when we took the city. Units of both advancing armies tried to thwart their strategy by pushing the Germans out of the city in many street battles. After several days, the Germans abandoned the southern part of Bydgoszcz, crossing the Brda River. The next day, our Eighth Regiment entered the fighting in the northwestern part of the city. We took many streets in fighting that lasted until late in the evening, contributing to the full liberation of Bydgoszcz. Then I followed many others into a brewery basement. The scene there was unforgettable. Over a floor littered with hundreds of broken liquor bottles and thousands of smashed cases of beer, hundreds of Polish and Soviet soldiers walked through a moving stream of alcohol, fumes alone seemingly capable of making one drunk. Everybody jostled one another to seize unbroken containers of alcohol. Among our spoils was an unbroken barrel of beer.

The next day we were ordered to move out in pursuit of the fleeing Germans. We moved very fast. In each village we passed north of Bydgoszcz, local people indicated that the Germans had left not long before. The farther away we were from the city, the shorter the time was since the Germans had left. We knew that very soon we would catch them, and soon we did. We were ready and eager for the encounter.

Near the village of Magdalenka, we spread out in an open field, which was snow covered and frozen. The best we could do for protection was to push up a little shield of snow in front of our heads, not much of a defense! Our goal was to move ahead and eject the enemy from the village, but this went very slowly, as we were met with heavy fire each time we raised our heads and tried to move. We quickly lay down again in the snow. After a few hours, our hands were so stiff with cold that we could not load our automatic weapons. Our situation was becoming desperate. Nevertheless, from time to time small units moved forward a little. At about two in the morning, we inched close to a barn from which the Germans were firing at us. A small artillery shell hit the place, setting the building on fire. That was a sign that encouraged us to launch a final attack. We stormed the village, firing as we advanced, and ejected the enemy from Magdalenka.

Then orders were given to rest for the remainder of the night. But before we dispersed into the village houses, we captured two military trucks loaded with boxes of chocolate. We picked out a few boxes, opened the barrel of beer from Bydgoszcz, and celebrated our victory with the village people. In recognition of our contribution to the liberation of Bydgoszcz and vicinity, we were renamed the "Eighth Bydgoszcz Regiment."

Early next morning we continued our advance. Many columns were moving across the snow-covered terrain. Close to us was a Soviet infantry column. At one point, a few figures with raised hands appeared in the field in front of us. We ran to pick them up, and found they were German soldiers from the Volksturm mobilization, most of them about fifty years old. They didn't want to fight anymore and decided to give themselves up. When we were leading the prisoners to turn them over to the staff command, a Soviet soldier came up from behind and shot them one by one. I picked up a Mauser rifle from one of them; I wanted to have such a nice weapon. A Soviet soldier asked me to show it to him. He took it and smashed on a nearby tree, breaking it in half. No hard feelings, I could go on without that rifle. The shooting of the prisoners was against the rules of war, and I did not condone it. Yet we should try to understand the state of mind of the soldier who killed them; he was relatively young and had probably been at war more than four years and taken part in many hellish battles in which hundreds and thousands of his comrades were killed by the Germans. He probably knew of the treatment of Soviet prisoners by the Nazis, conduct also far from the Geneva Convention's principles, and had seen the results of German atrocities against innocent civilians and the ruins of towns and villages. All this brutalized him as it did many others. War is brutal. Under such circumstances some soldiers were unable to distinguish between an armed or unarmed enemy. I had just seen one of them.

The First Polish Army was now moving in the first line of attack, posi-

tioned between the First and Second Belorussian Fronts, to the northwest of
Bydgoszcz, in the direction of Zlotow and Jastrowie. The army had to cover
nearly sixty miles in less than three days. The weather was bad; it was snowing and freezing. I remember that during the marches from Bydgoszcz to the
Jastrowie area, I learned to fall asleep on the frozen snow whenever there was
a short break. At the end of the break members of my platoon would call,
"Sergeant, get up! We're moving." After walking for a few minutes, I would
warm up and feel somewhat rested and able to continue. During the offensive, I'd been promoted to full sergeant.

The Third Division was assigned to the northern part of the front from
Koronowo toward Sepolno and Zlotow. On January 31, my regiment entered
the prewar territory of Germany. The division had to cross the Gwda River
on February 1. Things didn't go well for the regiment, which became disori-
ented in the snow-covered terrain, and lost contact with the rest of the advancing Polish Army. At one point, we were even counterattacked by the
Germans. I recall that our troops drew together defensively, feeling that we
were in a tight corner. We knew that in a few hours we had to go on the offensive, and I felt weak and apprehensive. My anxiety was probably the result
of the German attack, as we were accustomed to attacking them in the past
several months. A factor that I am certain influenced my unnecessary anxiety
was fear of falling into the hands of Germans. I was sure that if they discovered that I was Jewish I would not be well treated. I had heard that the Germans looked for commissars and Jews among Russian POWs. In that case
I could expect only pain and death. I had a similar feeling when I was in
Ivanovo, which was in danger of being overrun by the Germans in the fall
of 1941.

I took a large gulp of vodka to feel stronger and prepared for the worst. At
one point in the battle, instead of our battalion going forward, we got orders
to retreat from the bridgehead because our unit had run out of ammunition
and the Germans were attacking. The Gwda River was narrow at this point,
only about fifty yards wide. My platoon was in the rear guard that was supposed to hold at the riverbank against the attacking Germans on the other
side while the main force withdrew. The Germans approached the river, and
we came under heavy fire. We fired at them as well, man to man. It was a fierce
fight. In this action a complete and surprising change came over me. Instead
of fear, I felt a kind of joy that I was firing directly at approaching German

soldiers. I saw them coming and I took aim at them. Hadn't this been my wish all those years? My anger, accumulated over a long time, was suddenly released. That change from fear to calm confidence confirmed for me the many stories of heroic behavior by ordinary soldiers. One does not make a conscious decision to be a hero or to risk death. Every soldier wants both to strike the enemy and to survive. The dynamics of a battle and the circumstance in which each soldier finds himself generates action that may be called heroism, but that I would call the absence of fear and a strong desire to hit the enemy while there is a chance. If there was such an opportunity during my war with the Germans, this was it. In my case, I didn't feel heroic, just a change from fear to calm acceptance and then joy.

In the end we withstood the enemy pressure, held our position, and subsequently broke German resistance. We could then advance farther north. After taking the city of Jastrowie, the infantry battalions of the Eighth Regiment were withdrawn from combat at the front and sent back to liberated areas as garrison troops and to guard important industrial sites. My Third Battalion was sent initially to the city of Inowroclaw and thereafter to Bad Polzin (Polczyn Zdroj).

During the first half of February 1945, after my unit was withdrawn from the front lines for a short rest before taking up garrison duty, I was given leave to visit Lodz, which by a twist of fortune, I could not help liberate a few weeks before. I thumbed rides in military vehicles and reached Lodz in a few days. What I found was appalling. Wesola Street, where I had lived before escaping to the Soviet-occupied territories, was entirely empty; there was not a living soul around. There was a similar emptiness in many surrounding streets that were included in the ghetto. The ghetto was liquidated by the Germans in the fall of 1944.

Outside the ghetto walls, in non-Jewish neighborhoods, I heard reports that the Germans had taken the Jews to death camps; most often mentioned was Treblinka. I didn't have time to dig deeper into that tragedy. I had to return to my unit. What I had learned was devastating. I was not able to comprehend it. Even the Jewish cemetery at the end of Wesola Street was desecrated. The tombstones, instead of marking the places of eternal peace of the deceased, were now serving as sidewalks along the streets. The Nazis had not spared the dead, even taking from them their names. The entire ghetto was a huge cemetery, although without corpses. I felt that I could sense the ashes spreading from the crematorium of Treblinka, that I could see the smoky fire from the death camps, burning in the sky. There were many such places as Treblinka; I would learn about them as time went by.

Despite the rage and anguish that I felt, despite all I had learned, I still nurtured hope that some of my people would return. Not all concentration and death camps had yet been liberated. Maybe some of my loved ones managed to hide or were strong enough to survive. There still was time for them to come. I knew that my parents had left Wesola Street before the ghetto was closed in the beginning of 1940. They had moved to Kamiensk, where it may have been a little easier to survive. I expected that any survivors from my family would certainly return to Lodz and our former home.

On the floor of what had once been our room, many pieces of paper lay scattered. I looked through them for clues to what had happened. The only significant information was a letter from Mr. Zylberszatz, the neighbor with whom we escaped in 1939. He had left his wife and two daughters behind, intending to find a place to live in the Soviet-occupied city of Bialystok, then to return for them. It looked as if he had managed to come back, but it was not clear what then happened to them. The letter was addressed to the head of the ghetto, Mordechai Rumkowski, asking for a job as a guard. From that letter and other scraps of paper I guessed that the Zylberszatz family had occupied the room we lived in before the war. The only furniture left was our wardrobe. The wardrobe! When I left home in 1939 I hid on its top my collection of historical postcards depicting all forty Polish kings and famous Polish battles and their heroes, which schoolchildren assembled for history classes. What a surprise! Nobody had removed my treasure from the exact spot I had left it. Why was it still there? One possibility was that nobody looked at the top of the wardrobe, but I felt it was more likely that Zlata, one of Zylberszatz's daughters and who was my age, discovered it but decided to save it for me when I returned. That would have been a very kind gesture, and I was willing to believe it. I did not withdraw the treasure, assuming that it would be safer on top of the wardrobe than in the front lines.

I went down to the yard where in an extension of the main building a Jewish family had lived before the war. Their daughter Edzia worked with my sister Esther during the last fall I spent in Lodz. Edzia was a very attractive girl, with dark hair and soft brown eyes, a slender figure, and a beautiful friendly smile. She dressed like a lady from a wealthy home even though her parents were poor. I still remember Edzia dressed in a flared dark-blue winter coat, the collar adorned with gray astrakhan fur. Usually she went out with boyfriends who adored her, while I suffered pangs of jealousy. I was no match for her, since she was then eighteen years old while I was five years her junior. Nevertheless, I was privileged to be invited, or invited myself, to her room when her parents were away. We used to turn on the radio (a rarity in our building) and listen to beautiful dance music broadcast from Toulouse, France, in the dim room while Edzia lay on a couch. We didn't dance, because I didn't know how. No, Edzia wasn't there, there wasn't a living soul.

Even though I was attracted to Edzia, my true love was Lisowna, the other girl who worked in our room. Lisowna lived on Gdanska 31, more than a mile from my place. She was tall, blond, her face rather oval, with big blue eyes and a very sweet smile. Every evening after the girls finished working I volunteered to accompany her on the way home. For the adults I always had an excuse; usually I told my parents that I had to see a classmate about my homework. Naïve perhaps, but at that time it sounded convincing to me. I never told Lisowna how deeply I cared for her. It was a purely platonic love. I was happy just to walk with her. Now I went to Gdanska 31 alone, with a fearful heart. Lisowna was not there.

There were many other places I should have looked in the building at Wesola #8. Or in my uncle's place on Cegielniana 53. Another uncle had lived at Piotrkowska 88; and there was the Szrojt family at Narutowicza 12, and many others. But in addition to the short time available, I felt that I wanted to run away from the emptiness. It was a cemetery everywhere. My mind refused to accept the reality of the losses in my family and in all the other Jewish families I had known. I begged providence to give me at least one consolation, one known and loved face. I returned to my unit a broken man.

Between February and early April 1945, three important events happened to me. One of my company's tasks was to escort about two hundred German prisoners of war from an area somewhere near Kustrin (Kostrzyn), not far from the Oder River, to the city of Poznan, about eighty miles to the east. There we turned them over to Soviet military authorities who sent them to the Soviet Union. Nothing during all the war years gave me greater pleasure than escorting hundreds of German prisoners. Imagine, this little boy from Wesola Street was now leading a huge column of the *Herrenvolk* (master race) as prisoners, humiliated and subject to his command!

I enjoyed recalling when, at the beginning of the occupation, the Germans arrogantly insisted that everyone cross the Nowomiejska Street at the direction of their policemen. Now I ordered the POWs to form columns of four in a row, and they couldn't get it right for a long time. Were they that stupid? I was speaking in German, so they couldn't have claimed they didn't understand. They struck me as being quite dumb. No matter how many times I shouted at them to get four in a row, they still tried to form up in threes. Apparently, that was how they did it in the German army.

Oh, heavens! Why didn't my parents get the chance to see their little boy leading hundreds of their oppressors to the punishment they deserved? And that punishment was extremely mild in comparison to their crimes. How proud they would have been!

We continued from Poznan to Inowroclaw, about sixty miles northeast. Our Third Battalion was now positioned in Matwy, a suburb of Inowroclaw. A large chemical plant of the Solvay Company was located there. Less than ten miles away was the town of Kruszwica, with a large sugar plant, a source of supply for bootleg moonshine.

My best friend, Sergeant Feliks Kozlowski, used to bicycle there to pick up a few bottles of vodka. On one such ride, Feliks was killed under mysterious circumstances. There were no Germans around. His death shocked our battalion and was especially painful for me. He was of small stature, only eighteen years old, and very brave. I remembered the time we were together and surrounded by Germans. He advanced through some bushes to within four to five yards of them, without fear. Instead of turning and running, he went closer to the enemy and listened to what they were talking about. He did not understand what fear was. And now, instead of a hero's funeral, deputy battalion commander for political affairs Lieutenant Kowalczuk ordered that we bury him without ceremony or honors. Moreover, we were not allowed to see his body, raising suspicion that there was something to hide. Feliks did not commit any criminal act; his trip to Kruszwica was not forbidden. We were under loosened discipline and could move about without formal leave. It is still a mystery to me. I am convinced that there was foul play.

I must clarify here the role of political officers in the Polish Army. On the regimental level, political officers prepared field newsletters and made short announcements praising the heroism of units or individual soldiers. They delivered lectures during training or in preparation for battle. Infrequently they organized entertainment for the troops. The political officers preached the Communist political line but did not teach Communist doctrine as such. Their role in the Polish Army cannot be compared to the political commissars in the Soviet army. There, Communist Party cells were in operation and the party line was adhered to strictly. Frequently, Soviet army commissars tried to impose their authority over the military officers, often creating serious friction. In the Polish Army, political officers were much less intrusive. There were no political parties in the Polish Army, although Communists played a leading role.

Another event important for me was an incident with a priest in Bad Polzin (Polczyn Zdroj), a city in prewar Germany, northeast of Berlin. One evening I was on patrol in the city, as we were serving as its garrison, and I heard dramatic screaming and a call for help from a nearby Protestant church. I rushed inside to find a completely drunken Soviet soldier holding people at gunpoint, demanding cigarettes. The pastor, his wife, and some parishioners were on their knees, begging the soldier to let them go since they didn't have any cigarettes. Obviously, the soldier didn't understand what they were telling him in German, and even in Russian he wasn't able to comprehend much, since he was dead drunk. It took me a while to convince the soldier that these people had no cigarettes and that he should leave. As a result of my intervention in Russian, he did finally leave. Afterward, the people ran over to kiss my hand, thanking me for rescuing them from certain death. That's how they had seen their situation, judging perhaps from the behavior of German soldiers in similar situations.

I couldn't resist telling the pastor that I was Jewish and was happy to help them. Hearing this, the priest disappeared and returned after a few minutes with a book in Hebrew, reading from it and explaining the text. Of course, I understood the Hebrew text from the Old Testament without his translation. He was surprised that such a young soldier knew German, Russian, and Hebrew. And I certainly was pleased with and impressed by his gesture. We became good friends. I visited him as often as I could, and we had many interesting discussions. Even after the barbarism of the Nazis, I couldn't hate civilian Germans.

While in German towns, I had opportunities to speak with local people. Many times I heard that the SS had warned people that right behind the regular Soviet army were special Bolshevik-Jewish Battalions sent to kill them. I believe that the people in the church had the opportunity to learn first hand how false those stories were.

After a few weeks, we left Bad Polzin to continue the war with other Germans. We were now based close to the Oder River. The general offensive had stopped for a short period of consolidation and preparation for the final move toward Berlin and maybe the last battle of the war. Marshal Zhukov was now the general commander of the entire front. A leaflet was issued in his name, calling on the Polish troops to prepare for the decisive battle. We were situated in trenches, in miserable weather of freezing rain and snow that caused our coats to get wet and then freeze. I got a very high fever and was sent to the hospital. I therefore missed a few weeks of the final advance of my regiment. After my release from the hospital, I was sent to a reserve unit of the Polish Army in Warsaw. When I arrived as ordered, I asked the authorities to send me back to my original company.

In the meantime my regiment participated in encircling German units to the north and west of Berlin, thereby assisting the Soviet army in the final assault on Berlin. The Germans were still putting up a strong resistance, frequently counterattacking our units. Especially fierce fighting took place for the towns of Linum and Dechtow. There were many casualties in our regiment.

May 9, 1945, was Victory Day. On the way to my unit, I stopped in Lodz for a second time. The mayor of the city, Kazimierz Mijal, held a victory rally on Plac Wolnosci, the same place where, on September 1, 1939, I attended the rally when the Polish president announced Germany's aggression against Poland. So the tragic war that caused the world enormous losses in human life came to a victorious end. Lodz, my hometown, underwent a dramatic metamorphosis from a Socialist mayor in 1939 (Jan Kwapinski) through a fascist occupation and then a Communist mayor (Kazimierz Mijal). I did not wonder then where this change would lead. I was more interested in the consummation of the victory.

When I went again to Wesola Street in May 1945 I was thunderstruck. There were no houses left on the entire street! What had happened? How did the buildings disappear? There had been no fighting that could destroy an entire street. Later I learned that rumors spread that treasures had been hidden in the now-abandoned ghetto. Poles tore all those buildings apart in a search for the loot. By May 1945 the area was completely devastated in a shameful act of greed and disregard for the memory of their Jewish neighbors. My collection of postcards of Poland's history was also gone.

On the journey back to my Eighth Regiment, then stationed about twenty-five miles northwest of Berlin, I stopped in Berlin. It was probably May 11, 1945. It would be an understatement to say that I enjoyed standing on the streets of Berlin, the source of so much evil. How many times had we repeated the slogan, "Forward to Berlin," which was displayed everywhere? Now I had finally made it there, the Nazi enemy had been crushed, and our victory was complete. I was elated, thinking how many millions of people all over the world, especially those who were persecuted and murdered by the Nazis, had dreamt of victory over those monsters and of appropriate punishment for their misdeeds. Only few could let their dreams go as far as to imagine standing victorious in that city. How much I wished at that point to be able to tell my parents and siblings that I made it, that I had conquered the Nazis, and that I was standing in the richly deserved ruins of Berlin.

I owed my personal victory to the millions who fell in battle. I owed it to millions of soldiers in the Soviet army, to the Polish and allied armies. Regardless of the Soviet regime, I had a debt to that land and especially its warm and generous people, who had let me live among them and who had provided me with the automatic rifle I used to fight the Nazis. I owed gratitude to the many nations that supplied our fighters with arms, ammunition, food, and clothing. And I was grateful for the camaraderie and mutual support among soldiers of different ethnic and religious backgrounds in my Polish Army. Not only was Nazism defeated in that war, but likewise, I thought, the anti-Semitism that prevailed in prewar Poland. This was new, it was born here, in this army, and was the foundation of my belief that a new Poland would be home to all its citizens.

My personal victory was also the result of sheer luck. Many times I was in a situation when a comrade fell in battle nearby and it could have been me. I thought often of such cases while I was in Berlin. Like in a fast-moving film, I ran through in my memory all the thousands of miles I'd covered on foot during the war to reach this point. I remembered the hundreds of nights during which my eyes searched the darkness, guarding our positions, stretching my nerves to the utmost. I had to endure cold, frost, rain, dirt, fatigue, and even hunger, the agony of failure and defeat. All of it and much more were part of the price paid to defeat Nazism.

In Moscow, at ten in the evening on May 9, 1945, Stalin ordered a victory salute by firing thirty artillery salvos from one thousand guns. Hurray!

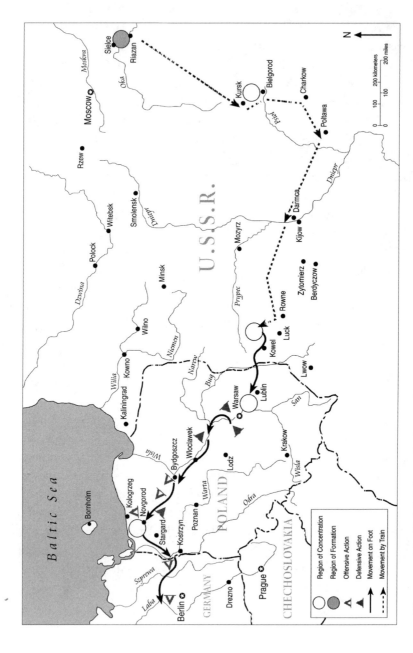

6. War route of the Eighth Infantry Regiment of the Polish army

Adam Broner in front of the Kremlin, Moscow, 1954.

Broner's late wife, Zina, with their two sons, Walter (*left*) and Edward (*right*), 1965.

Broner's brother Samuel and his wife, Bronia, daughter Mary, and son Simon, 1965.

Broner in uniform, circa 1945.

The restored Kosciuszko monument on the Freedom Plaza (Plac Wolnosci) in Lodz, which was demolished on November 11, 1939, by the German occupiers.

Adam and Barbara Broner in Florida.

18
War after Victory

After a few weeks, we began to prepare to return to Poland. By the end of May 1945, we were ready for the journey, and this time not on foot. The train we boarded stopped frequently at railway stations where we visited the cafeteria and enjoyed a break from military rations. In many cases, railroad workers offered soldiers a drink and held impromptu rallies to welcome the victorious Polish Army. On one such occasion, I consumed too much vodka, returned to the train, and passed out on the coupling that joined two cars together. I don't remember anything after that; my comrades brought me inside the car. I don't usually drink too much, but as a victorious soldier, I couldn't refuse the drinks offered by the railroad workers.

We reached Lublin and continued on foot toward Krasnik. On the way, we spent a night in Majdanek, in empty barracks at the infamous German death camp. Many thousands perished in that place, their bodies burned in the crematorium or dumped in mass graves. How could our leaders be so insensitive to the feelings of the soldiers, whose parents, relatives, and friends may have died there too? I could not sleep that night. I wandered around and was glad to leave the next morning.

In Krasnik, a small town in the Lublin district, we were billeted in prewar barracks that remained in relatively good shape. The building looked grim to me, especially after the night in Majdanek. Toward evening, we were given leave and could meet civilians in the city. The local population threw many parties for the victorious soldiers. Everywhere the reception was enthusiastic. There was also an event organized by Jewish survivors, and many Jewish soldiers attended. Despite the festive atmosphere, we heard many tragic stories about the plight of Jews murdered in death camps. The survivors attending the party had been interned mostly in smaller camps in the southeast of Poland. Apparently the Nazis did not have time to liquidate them. We could not get a complete picture of what happened to the majority of Jews in Poland and in Europe. Some of the camps had been liberated only a few months or even few weeks earlier, therefore, the full dimensions of the Jewish tragedy were not yet known. Even less was known about the scale of the loss of Poland's population, both Christians and Jews.

I met a fellow named Yankel, who was among the hosts and as it turned out would play an important role in my life. I also noted with interest at the party the speed with which the survivors of various ghettoes and concentration camps regained their equilibrium and vigorously and successfully pursued a new life. I started to date a very attractive young lady, the owner of a shoe store. One evening we were to have dinner together. Suddenly we heard commotion on the first floor, and then on the stairs leading to the living quarters above the shop. The lady turned toward the sound and fell into the arms of the man who entered. It was her husband returning from a concentration camp; there went my date! Obviously, I was happy for them, and we remained good friends for the time I was in Krasnik.

Normally, the return of soldiers from a victorious war would have been a very happy and peaceful one. But these were not peaceful times in Poland. The struggle between the old and new was far from settled. As it turned out, this period in my military service was, in many respects, worse than the war against the Germans.

These were the first months of the newly established and Communist-dominated administration in Poland. In addition to the Polish Workers Party (PPR, Communist), the prewar Polish Socialist Party (PPS), the Peasants' Party (SL), and Labor Party (SP) created a governing coalition. The PPR and PPS were the leading groups in the coalition. The Socialists, although numerically strong and with a long tradition in Poland, played a secondary role. After a few years their party was absorbed into the Polish United Workers Party (PZPR) and ceased to exist.

Important forces in Poland that resisted the new authorities were the remnants of the Home Army (AK) and its sympathizers, as well as the semi-fascist National Armed Forces (NSZ). Initially, a large segment of the population supported the opposition. Harsh persecution by the Soviets and the Polish administration of Home Army members created a renewed underground of former members and allies of the AK. In addition, in the territories along the new eastern frontiers of Poland, a sizable Ukrainian nationalist force began terrorist attacks against the new administration.

Not long after our return from Germany, we began our new war, this time with the Ukrainian nationalist movement, the Home Army, and the NSZ. We were now undertaking a different role than that for which the Polish Army was ostensibly created—defending the nascent Communist regime. During the war with Germany we were not told that such an assignment was waiting for us. The political leadership of the army and its creator Stalin well knew that there would be resistance to the establishment of a Communist regime in Poland, and that the Soviet army would need a Polish force to protect it. My impression was that during the war the Kosciuszko Army was used sparingly against the Nazis, in order to preserve it for its coming domestic role. The Soviets understood that if the Red Army were assigned to pacify Poland, resistance would be more widespread, stronger, and more dangerous. I should add that there was historic animosity between Poles and Russians, who had been fighting each other throughout their history. This was a significant factor that the Soviets had to reckon with in the process of imposing a Communist regime in Poland.

Four divisions of the Polish Army were assigned to the Lublin and Rzeszow districts, where most of those underground resistance units operated. On June 13, 1945, the Third Battalion, including my Seventh Company, was ordered to leave Krasnik and move to the city of Bilgoraj to initiate a campaign against the armed opposition.

Before the war Bilgoraj was largely inhabited by Jews. It was a very conservative town, with Jewish customs unaltered for hundreds of years. Nobel Laureate Isaac Bashevis Singer described a visit to Bilgoraj before the first world war in these words: "I had a chance to see our past as it really was. Time seemed to flow backward. I lived Jewish history." Now history had swept it all away with one rough stroke. Most of the Jews perished during the war, and even if someone had survived, it became too dangerous for Jews to live there. The few surviving Jews from the Bilgoraj region were now in Krasnik, where we had been based a few days earlier. Bilgoraj was a ghost town.

Across from the barracks where my company was located was a temporary Soviet army hospital. I had the pleasure of getting acquainted with a Russian nurse who worked there. She was blonde, with blue eyes, a nice smiling face, tall, and with a beautiful figure; a real *Ruskaya krasavica* (Russian beauty). It was easy to get to see her, as their building was right across the way, and when she appeared in the evening I made sure that I was there, too. After several trysts, we noticed that a group of young boys had discovered our secluded meeting place, so we had to conduct a little shadow war with the youngsters. It was rather a sweet war, yet we had to change position a few times in order to outwit our pursuers. At last we could declare victory.

From a military point of view, the threat from Ukrainian fighters was much more dangerous than from the Polish underground. Politically, however, the Polish underground was considered a far more serious adversary. The Ukrainians were organized as the UPA (Ukrainian Insurrection Army). During the war, many Ukrainians collaborated with the Germans, who promised them an independent state. Ukrainian collaborators committed many atrocities against Poles and Jews (and other Ukrainians) on behalf of the Nazis. After the war, Ukrainians resisted Polish authorities who sought to repatriate them to the Soviet Union, where they knew they would not be warmly welcomed if not persecuted. Officially, the authorities claimed the repatriation was intended to unite the Ukrainian population with their brethren. In reality, we were seizing Ukrainians against their will, locking them in railroad cars, and sending them across the border.

We would enter a Ukrainian or mixed Polish-Ukrainian village and attempt to convince the Ukrainians to leave within a week voluntarily. A day or two before the week was up, we would return to the village and if we did not see any preparations, we would load their belongings onto a cart and take them to the railway station. There we locked the people into the cars, guarding them until they left.

What sometimes happened was tragic and inhumane. The night after the Ukrainians were sent away, and after we left the emptied village, bands of Ukrainian guerillas set fire to all the buildings in the village, whether or not Polish or mixed Polish-Ukrainian families were still there. Terrible suffering resulted from such wholesale arson. The UPA guerillas would often attack the railroad station, free the people from the locked railroad cars, and take them to the forest. On occasion they also attacked the military units that were carrying out the expulsions.

On December 4, 1945, I was on orderly duty in the battalion kitchen in Horyniec. The entire Third Battalion of our Eighth Regiment was moving from that village to Kocury. My duty was to make sure that a hot meal was prepared and delivered to our new location. The kitchen was to remain in Horyniec until the evening when the cooking was completed.

We were almost ready to move when the first news arrived of a horrible disaster. Before reaching Kocury, the commander called all unit officers to the head of the column to deliver some last-minute instructions. At that moment, a hail of fire was launched at the entire column from the little hills surrounding the country road. Many casualties resulted. The commander of my platoon, Lieutenant Matejko Franciszek, was killed instantly, along with several other officers, including Captain Zastocki, the deputy battalion commander. My company commander, Lieutenant Jan Sakowicz, was severely wounded. It was one of the worst encounters with the UPA.

Our regiment's female officers fought bravely during the war with the Germans. One of them, Lieutenant Maria Gorniak, commanded a platoon of heavy machine guns, and she was always brave and had a smile even in the most difficult situations. Now Maria was crying convulsively over the body of Captain Zastocki, who we expected was planning to marry her. Love overcomes courage.

On March 9, 1946, a large group of about five hundred UPA fighters (including women) attacked the Third Battalion in the village of Lubycza-Krolewska, in the southeastern part of present-day Poland, not far from the Soviet border. It was a very dark night. The UPA attacked our outposts around the village and the railroad station, where cars were loaded with repatriates. They succeeded in taking out our outposts and then advanced toward the heart of the village where the regimental command was located. The guerrillas attacked several buildings where soldiers and officers were sleeping. The regimental commander, Colonel Zielenin, miraculously escaped through a window. The situation was critical since it was not clear to the rest of us where the enemy or the friendly forces were. A few junior officers in the room we shared panicked. No wonder, as we had seen atrocities perpetrated by the UPA. They would mutilate captured soldiers, often sawing their bodies into pieces. Most soldiers and officers grabbed weapons and ran out into the street. Soon, there was a sizable group of us advancing toward the area where we heard gunfire.

After a bit, we became aware of a group of fighters cautiously moving toward us between the buildings, taking up a position about ten yards away. At any moment they or we would start shooting and there would be a massacre. This was one of those moments when one move could make an enormous difference. I called to the other group to identify itself. If it was a friendly group, we were safe; if it was the enemy, then a barrage of fire would be directed at the caller and the rest of us. Though risky, it was still better than to start shooting immediately. Our deputy battalion commander, who was leading the other group, recognized my voice. He then let the whole group know that we were friendly, and we advanced together against our real enemy. After we succeeded in pushing out the UPA band, the officer had many kind words for my conduct. Although I was recommended for a decoration for this action, I never received it. I did have a medal for valor in combat, for an action several months earlier.

Those were not the worst moments of my war after the victory. I recall with horror the guard duty I spent on a bridge about two miles from the battalion bivouac. I was out there alone in the darkness of the night. Any attempt to destroy the bridge by the Ukrainians, a frequent objective of theirs, would have spelled my end, and just as dangerous would have been their desire to take a Polish soldier prisoner. To this day, I do not understand why the practice of maintaining guard at various points in a friendly garrison was applied in this dangerous place. A sufficient force should have been deployed to protect the bridge while sending for help, as was the rule elsewhere in our campaign.

The Polish underground, mainly NSZ, attacked officials of the new regime, which they considered Communist and acting on behalf of the Soviet Union. The NSZ also targeted Jews. Their slogan was "Poland without Jews." That was my wake-up call to postwar reality. My view, or hope, that ethnic hatred had been eradicated was clearly premature. One could have expected that after the Germans murdered more than three million Polish Jews, even the most hardheaded and ardent anti-Semite should have been satisfied. Apparently, they were not.

A large part of our effort was to convince farmers to give up weapons they were hiding and sometimes using at night in operations against the new government. A different strategy was applied to NSZ forces that were not amenable to persuasion. When ordered on a special action, we would surround a selected village and detain all men for interrogation in order to find guerillas. Then we also combed nearby forests in search of the underground fighters.

In one of our forays into the forest to capture a band operating in that area, we found a ramshackle hut in the middle of the forest. As we approached it, a young girl ran into the shack. It did not seem suspicious to us; she could have been scared at seeing so many soldiers. We spent some time talking with the owner and then left.

I used to talk with a friendly peasant living near my billet in Bilgoraj. Since I was stationed near his house, it was natural for him to talk to a neighbor. During my visits he was very careful; whenever he talked to me, he always did some work, making my presence seem less suspicious. When I visited the friendly peasant the day after our encounter at the hut, what he told me was a revelation. First of all he knew everything about the previous day's patrol into the forest. More important, he told me that just as we arrived, a group of about twenty guerillas had run out the back and hid in the bushes behind the building. The girl whom we saw run into the place warned them to escape. What good luck! This time they had decided not to put up a fight. If so, both sides could have been in big trouble.

In another raid on the resistance, we were more successful. We captured an AK group in the forest that didn't have time to escape. I captured a very nice young man, who did not look like the stereotyped guerilla. After a few days, he was released from detention and told me many stories of his life. We became friends. There were many such small groups that avoided attacking the new Polish government. Most of them stayed in forests after the war as they feared being rounded up by the Soviets and sent to Siberia. Such was the fate of higher-ranking AK officers, and was feared by all AK members. To be on the safe side, many who had previously left the underground had recently returned to the forests. The man I captured was one of those.

In order to avoid an escalation of the conflict, the new Polish government tried to persuade such opponents to surrender voluntarily, promising not to prosecute them. In a few cases, this policy was successful. In one case, the guerillas surrendered on condition that a government of national unity be formed, which did occur at the beginning of August 1945. Another positive example was the negotiated surrender of a large group of AK fighters under the command of "Zapora," the pseudonym of Major Heronim Dekutowski. Negotiations started on the level of our battalion, and in the final phase were transferred to the Third Division. As a result, a predominant part of the fighters in Dekutowski's group decided to turn in their weapons.

In the beginning of 1946 the first group of soldiers and junior officers were demobilized. Some of my friends settled in a small town not far from our unit's location. One day I was invited to visit them. The party was in a nice apartment, with many lights aglow, a strong contrast with the darkness usual in the military. Tables were loaded with food, reminding me of a Jewish holiday, such as Passover. I had planned to stay overnight, and as always I had my automatic weapon with me, which I put it in a corner of the room where I was to sleep. For no reason, during the evening I suddenly felt the urge to commit suicide, to take the weapon and shoot myself! After a few seconds I was able to push the impulse out of my mind. I wondered, why the sudden depression? Was it the contrast between my life in the army, the uncertainty over when and how it would end for me, and the brightly illuminated, festive atmosphere and peaceful family life I witnessed now?

In April 1946, it was my turn to be demobilized. I was offered an opportunity to become a career officer, but that didn't appeal to me. I began to prepare for civilian life, but I had not the slightest idea what I was going to do. That seemed secondary to my immediate concern of getting safely out of the region where the NSZ was still operating. I'd heard stories of the NSZ forcing Jews out from trains and killing them.

My father's name was Israel, which was very easy to recognize as a Jewish name, even if my appearance didn't indicate that I was a Jew. Therefore I asked a friend in the regimental personnel office to enter my name on my discharge papers as "Adam son of Jozef," instead of "son of Israel." Military documents prepared before my discharge, including for the award of my medal, still listed my father's correct name, Israel. Later, in civilian life, I repaired the dual names. With a new name, I had a good chance to get through an NSZ checkpoint, although I would still be considered suspect because of my military uniform, which they didn't like either.

I left my unit one afternoon after friendly farewells from my comrades. A soldier was assigned a horse cart to drive me to the railway station. Suddenly, I felt defenseless without my automatic rifle or revolver. What an irony! After all those years of fighting against fascists, I had to face similar enemies in my liberated country. It was in sharp contrast to the expectation I had and to the future promised by the Communist leadership of my army. It was not their fault. In opposing the regime the Communists were instituting in Poland, the NSZ was also turned to a campaign of terror against the few remaining Jews who could still be found in Poland.

Although I was warned about the danger of being killed by the NSZ if they discovered my Jewish origin, I was not aware of the extent of the perils emanating from the Polish population at large. About the time I was discharged from the army, Jews were being murdered quite frequently.

On February 17, 1945, a Pole in Sokoly, Poland, murdered seven Jews, including a small orphan girl. In May 1945, Poles murdered four Jews who re-

turned home to Dzialoszyce. On August 11, 1945, anti-Jewish riots erupted in
Krakow. On October 25, 1945, Jews were attacked in Sosnowiec; on November 19, 1945, anti-Jewish riots took place in Lublin. On March 19, 1946, one of
two survivors of the Belzec death camp was murdered in Lublin after his tes-
timony about the horrors in that camp. On March 28, 1946, Jews traveling
from Krakow to Lodz were tortured and murdered by Poles; on April 30, 1946,
seven Jews were murdered in Nowy Targ. On July 4, 1946, a pogrom took place
in the city of Kielce, under the pretext that Jews had abducted a Christian boy
for ritual murder. The next day the boy was found unharmed at the house of
a friend he had gone to visit in a nearby village. On July 11, 1946, Polish pri-
mate August Cardinal Hlond blamed the Jews for the anti-Semitic riots in
Kielce. In a short period after the Nazis were driven out of Poland, forty-two
Jews were murdered and many more injured, among them soldiers of the Polish Army.

When I was driven to the railway station after being discharged from the
army, I was not aware of the crimes perpetrated by Poles on Jews after the
war. Army newsletters did not mention them. Even later, not all those crimes
were reported in official newspapers. When I learned about the Kielce pogrom, news of which could not be suppressed, I could not comprehend nor
accept that this was happening in the country I had promised to liberate. How
can one explain such behavior of people in a country in which six million of
its inhabitants were murdered by the Nazis? Wasn't it proper to at least mourn
the deaths of three million Jewish countrymen? Though one could admit that
a significant number of Poles did not like Jews and should not expect them
to lament their deaths, such lack of sympathy should not lead to murder of
the handful of survivors who returned to Poland. The perpetrators were determined to complete what the German Nazis had not been able to accomplish. Some of these atrocities were caused by fear that surviving Jews might
ask for return of their apartments, furniture, and other belongings they had
to abandon while fleeing the Nazis.

Those events cast serious doubt in my mind whether I was right to claim
that I had won the war against Nazism and anti-Semitism when I stood on
the streets of Berlin. When I was preparing to leave my army unit, I was
shaken to learn of NSZ attacks upon Jews. When I went back to Lodz and
learned more about the atrocities and especially the Kielce pogrom perpetrated by ordinary Poles, I was terrified.

I did not regret what I did in the army after returning to Poland. I could not choose what I wanted to do. It was army discipline. However, I can justify as necessary the struggle against the NSZ, as I saw it as a violent leftover of prewar extreme right-wing and fascist groups. I was much less happy with the campaign against the remnants of AK. But we never had an open fight with them. The AK never initiated a skirmish with the Polish Army. The forest was a sanctuary for the AK, protecting them from arrest by Polish or Soviet authorities.

The NSZ concentrated on murdering Jews and members of the militia and secret police. They were quite successful in places where there were no strong government forces. I do not recall any fighting with the NSZ while I was still in the army.

The war with the Ukrainians in the UPA was a different story. I don't know if they would have been as hostile and aggressive if the Poles had not tried to repatriate them to the Soviet Union. What the Polish Army was doing was according to an agreement with the Soviets, but that does not justify or diminish its cruelty. We tried to convince them to leave Poland voluntarily. But in the end we pushed them out. I was not happy with that operation. But I had no choice.

Now that I was a civilian, I could choose to stay in Poland or to flee again. At the beginning of the German occupation in 1939, my instinct told me to escape from the Germans. I saw the danger coming from the Nazis. Now, having good reason to be disillusioned, why did I not again reach the conclusion that it was dangerous to stay in Poland? Many young Polish Jews were leaving the country for Palestine, the obvious place for Jews to reestablish their ancient homeland. Yet I decided to stay.

My service in the army instilled in me two beliefs that helped me arrive at this decision. The first one was that I felt I was co-owner of the land for which I had fought and in a sense was responsible for the direction it would take. Second, I believed in the principles that were enunciated and effectuated in the army as the foundation of the new Poland. I was not a believer in the Communist system that I had observed and experienced in the Soviet Union, but I believed in brotherhood, equality, and justice for all. The treatment I received from the Soviet authorities in Siberia clearly contradicted those ideals.

I believed in the ideas I learned before the war from the Polish Socialist

Party. I recalled the opposition of the PPS to the right-wing National Demo-
crats, which preached virulent anti-Semitism. To every proclamation of the
ND the PPS responded with vigorous condemnation. I would compare the
PPS posters, with black letters on a red background, with those of the ND,
which used red letters on white, the Polish national colors. With great satis-
faction, I observed that the PPS was true to its Socialist principles. Politically,
it was not an easy strategy for the PPS, since a large percentage of the Polish
population had not been freed from its anti-Semitic virus.

The ND was not satisfied with propaganda alone; it frequently turned to
violence. Often, young anti-Jewish militants would beat up Jews sitting in
parks on Saturday afternoons or on any other convenient occasion. During
the municipal elections of 1938 groups of ND members amused themselves
by threatening Jews with knives; one day, *Pani* Sabina, our Polish landlady,
returned from a walk horrified by the violence she had just witnessed. "*Jesu
Maria*," she cried, "they're using such big knives against the Jews," indicating
the knives were as big as her forearm. Despite the efforts of the ND to weaken
the PPS, the Socialists won that election.

In 1939, the central government forbid the customary May Day demonstrations in the streets, but rallies could be held indoors. By that time, I was a
partisan of the Polish Socialist Party. I decided to attend a May Day rally at
the Zacheta movie theater on Zgierska Street, not far from my home. There
for the first time I heard hundreds of Polish workers singing the proletarian
anthem "The International." I would sing this song many more times, but it
never was as inspiring as at that rally. I was too young to join the Socialist
Party, but intuitively I saw them as an honorable movement, with principles
I learned from their proclamations posted on the streets against the hatred
and anti-Semitism of the ND Party. These political issues, which I did not
understand fully at the time, created a foundation that later in my life became
central to my beliefs.

Most important, I considered the attack on Jews after the Holocaust as part
of an attack on the new regime, which was in its initial phase of formation. I
believed that it would lead to a democratic country with a pluralistic political
system. I believed that the new structure would grant equal rights to all citizens. The Polish Socialist Party that I admired before the war was playing a
significant role in establishing that new system. It was easy for me to see the
attacks on Jews as a continuation of the prewar ND program with its virulent
anti-Semitism. The new Poland was on my side, while the Jews' murderers

were a remnant of the past that, with time, would be eradicated. I believed that the new principles would ultimately prevail. My allies were the Polish Army and the authorities who took power in Poland. I still believed in them. I remained a fighter. I had to rise above the scum. The war was still going on, and I would participate, if by different means.

3
Stages of New Life

19
Return to Lodz

After my discharge from the army in April 1946, I returned to Lodz. The city looked strange. All the familiar faces were gone. Enough time had passed for the city to recover from the war and for the survivors to return. No one from my family was among the few thousand Jews who came back to Lodz. My hopes for a miracle, that I would see them again, still occupied my dreams at night and my thoughts when awake. Unfortunately, it became abundantly clear that almost all the Jewish communities of Eastern and Central Europe had been annihilated. The life, tradition, culture, and vitality of millions of Jews who lived in that part of the world were eradicated. It was not a temporary loss that could be restored; never would that Jewish life reappear in this part of the world, or for that matter, anywhere else.

While wandering in the city, looking for the familiar among the new, I happened to find myself on Kamienna Street. Before the war this street was a residential area situated between poorer and more affluent neighborhoods. Yet it also had the reputation as a place frequented by prostitutes and their clients. After the war, Kamienna Street became a haven for low-class prostitutes. Yet it was to play a significant role in the next several years in my life. In the late 1930s I had delivered hats that my father manufactured to the Hochenberg store on Kamienna #2. I was curious to see if they had survived.

As I came to the old store, from across the street at Kamienna #3 a loud voice called me. It was Yankel, the fellow from Krasnik whom I had met at the victory party for soldiers in June 1945. After a warm greeting, and then learning I had no place to stay, Yankel offered me a share in his room, also occupied by three young women. I accepted gladly. Yankel and his girlfriend moved to

another apartment in the same building, leaving me to share a room with
Bronia and Basia.

Bronia offered to introduce me to Sulecki, a weaver and political activist
in the textile mill where she worked. Before the war, Mr. Levin owned the
mill, but it was taken over by the government after Levin did not appear to
claim his property. It was then difficult to get a job in Lodz unless one had a
Communist or Socialist activist as a sponsor. Sulecki was a perfect choice. He
was a longtime prewar Polish Communist, and he had spent several years in
jail with Jewish Communists. While in jail he learned to speak perfect Yiddish. Comrade Sulecki made sure that I was hired as his assistant weaver. After a few weeks I was working independently on two looms. I worked there
for about a year, during which the administration of the mill and the so-
called workers' government squeeze more output from the workers without
increasing, and sometimes even reducing, wages. Several strikes were organized to demand more pay and a better food supply. The government used
its propaganda machine and party activists to defuse the unrest.

In my wandering about the city, I ran into David, my roommate from
Novosibirsk in 1940–41. He invited me to stay with him and his wife in a room
at the other end of Kamienna Street. He had recently married a very pretty
young girl. The couple slept in a bed in the single room, while I had comfortable bedding on the floor. The trouble was that he had to leave for work very
early in the morning, while I was left with his beautiful wife. After a few days
he considered my presence there a danger to his marriage—without reason,
but understandably—and I had to find another place. I went back to Bronia's
room. Her roommate Basia decided to join her sister in a nearby building,
presumably to create a more private space for Bronia and me. Bronia's cousin,
who visited her occasionally, began to hint of a marriage for the two of us.
However, my desire was to establish myself and find a career since I considered work in the textile mill only as a way station toward an unknown future.

Late in the summer of 1946 my brother Sam took advantage of a repatriation agreement between the Polish and Soviet governments and returned to
Lodz. Our reasoning that led us to accept Soviet passports in 1941 had proven
to be correct. Intuitively we thought that the situation after the war would
be conducive to return to our country. Back in our city he wandered about
the same way I had. The first place he went was Wesola Street where we lived
before the war. But our street did not exist anymore. Then he went to the
Jewish Committee where all returning survivors left messages and searched

for relatives and friends. There were hundreds of messages on a billboard looking for survivors. The best way to get information was by meeting directly with other survivors. A typical conversation would go like this: "What camp were you in?" Hearing the answer, then, "Oh, my sister was there, did you by chance meet her?" Or, "What ghetto were you in, and until when?" Such inquiries sometimes yielded stunning information. My brother found me through David, the fellow from Novosibirsk whom I had briefly lived with on Kamienna Street. One shining morning a knock at the door awakened me. Bronia opened the door and there he was—Sam back in Lodz! We were reunited after many years.

Matters then developed very fast. Bronia and Sam fell in love and decided to marry as soon as he could establish himself and earn some money. I was very happy for them. I then moved to a special boardinghouse for young survivors, the Bursa, organized by the Jewish Committee. There I met an enthusiastic group of young people, most of whom had already resumed their education, some in high school and others at the University or Polytechnic. Inspired by this atmosphere, I decided to restart my own education. Within two years I finished high school and in the fall of 1948 was admitted to the Chief Commercial School in Warsaw (*Szkola Glowna Handlowa w Warszawie*), which had a branch campus in Lodz. I did not do that well during my first year there, mainly because I had to work for a living and my job was very demanding. I rarely attended classes, and my education was in real danger.

Political developments from 1946 to 1949 were designed by the authorities to establish a Soviet regime in Poland. The first important act was the holding of a referendum in June 1946, in which citizens were asked to vote yes or no to three propositions: Are you in favor of abolishing the Senate? Are you in favor of agricultural reform and nationalization of the major Polish industries? Are you in favor of establishing the country's western borders on the Baltic and the Oder and Neisse rivers? Army units formed political brigades to work to promote a yes vote on all three questions. This was clear use of the army for political purposes and agitation, a role never stated as a mission during the war. I was not part of this as I had already left the army.

Not only the army but civilian political activists and groups also were active to make sure the "three times yes" campaign won. It was widely known that a number of activists voted many times to ensure the result. The Polish Peasants Party associated with Deputy Prime Minister Stanislaw Mikolajczyk recommended a no vote on the first question and the NSZ called for rejection of all three proposals. Both workers' parties, the PPS and the Communist PPR, urged a yes vote on all three questions. Not surprisingly the yes votes won, as there were widespread irregularities at the voting places and falsification of the results.

Since the Polish Peasants Party had a large following, especially among the rural population, it constituted a formidable opposition to the sovietization of Poland. The Communists decided to reduce PPP influence before the general election scheduled for January 1947. It started an intense campaign against Mikolajczyk and his party, portraying them as reactionaries working against the government's efforts to lift the national standard of living. The PPP candidates for parliament were prevented from campaigning. The result of the fraudulent election was 394 parliament seats for the Communist coalition and only twenty-eight for the Peasants Party. Few people believed that was an honest result. In October 1947, in danger of being arrested, Mikolajczyk escaped from Poland, assisted by the U.S. embassy, and settled in the United States. The Polish government in exile considered Mikolajczyk a traitor for his association with the Polish coalition government; Mikolajczyk's Peasants Party was near collapse after he fled. Without the PPP the government had no organized internal opposition.

In the fall of 1946 I found my way to a study group organized by the Jewish socialist party, the Bund. There were interesting lectures on ancient history and Jewish literature. These courses led me to the youth organization of the Bund, *Cukunft* (the Future). The Bund had a long history of activity in Russia since the end of the nineteenth century. Politically it was to the right of the Communists, and the Bolsheviks in Russia considered them inimical to their rule. In 1940 they lured Bund leaders to Moscow, where they were arrested and subsequently killed. After the war, the Bund reestablished itself in Poland. The increasingly Communist-dominated regime in Poland created mortal danger for the Bund and *Cukunft*.

Having taken care of the open opposition, the Polish Workers Party turned to preparing itself for further power. In the summer of 1948 it began a purge in both "workers parties," removing members that demonstrated sympathy to the West. Bund members considered the climate increasingly dangerous, and one happy day its leadership and many activists escaped from Poland. In the Bursa my roommate was Avreml Zheleznikov, the leader of *Cukunft* in Lodz. He also disappeared. Initially it was not clear what happened to him and many other Bund leaders and activists. After a few days rumors confirmed that they had successfully crossed the Polish border and were on their way to Paris. I knew that Zheleznikov had permission to carry a weapon, since leaders of left-wing parties and some Jews were in danger of being assaulted by the NSZ. I looked for my roommate's weapon and found a TT revolver under the pillow on his bed. I had such a revolver when I was in the army and wanted to have it now as well. I expected that the secret police would soon be searching the room; nevertheless, I hid it under my pillow. It was not a smart move, but my desire to have a weapon prevailed. A few days later an official of the Bursa and a secret police officer searched my room and found the revolver. I explained that I had no idea that it was hidden there.

Pressure was put on the youth organizations of political parties to join the Association of Polish Youths (ZMP). Over time ZMP became a mass youth organization of several million members. Even though the ZMP became the youth section of the United Workers Party, which was clearly Communist, it would not be correct to consider several million ZMP members as Communists. The majority still went to church and celebrated religious holidays, and few accepted Communist doctrine. Most ZMP members were reluctant to attend Communist indoctrination sessions, and the ZMP's leadership stressed general patriotic and educational themes and organized entertainment events to attract and retain young members. Young people joined the ZMP mostly for opportunistic reasons such as having a better chance for admission to institutions of higher learning or to go to summer camp. Only among the members of ZAMP, a suborganization for youth who were enrolled in institutions of higher education, did serious political indoctrination take place. ZAMP became the source of young Communist Party membership.

A few months after the foundation of the ZMP, the secretary general of the Polish Workers Party, Wladyslaw Gomulka, was expelled from the party for "right-wing and nationalist deviation." Boleslaw Bierut, the nominal president of Poland, who supposedly was not affiliated with any party, replaced Gomulka as party chief. Bierut began a farm collectivization program and liquidated the PPS through rapid "unification" of the two workers' parties. Also at the initiative of Bierut, Soviet marshal Konstanty Rokossovsky was invited to take over Poland's Ministry of National Defense. This was followed by a purge in the army and a series of trials of leading Polish generals, who were charged with spying for Great Britain and the CIA and plotting to overthrow the government. The hand of the Soviet secret police and its methods of concocting accusations, torturing its victims, and holding show trials were clearly visible.

During those years as the Communists consolidated their hold on power, thousands of AK members were arrested and sent to Siberia. All news information and print material was censored. The spread of state terror led to fear and conformism. Part of the intellectual community went over to the Communists and helped the party spread its ideology. A significant part of the population, having no choice, became opportunists. Even if the majority of the population was not convinced that the Communist government led the nation in the right direction it went along because no other options remained. Poles then longed to rebuild the country after the tremendous devastation of the war. As the government presented ambitious plans that promised to improve the economy, many willingly participated in that effort. However, the nationalization of all industries including retail trade, fiscal pressure on small private enterprises, and forced collectivization of agriculture impeded food production. State economic plans, especially the Six-Year Plan of 1949–55, directed the country toward the development of heavy industries and the production of military supplies. Both the agrarian policy and the prioritizing of heavy and military industries created severe shortages of food. Naturally this led to disappointment and resentment, which found its outlet in the riots of June 1956 in Poznan.

20
Moscow
The Center of Indoctrination

During the summer of 1949 several students living in the Bursa dormitory were offered a stipend to study in the Soviet Union. I did not apply, for fear the Soviet authorities would dig out my record of misbehavior in the years 1940–43. However, by the end of the recruiting period the Polish Ministry of Higher Education had a shortage of approved candidates. They were in a hurry for candidates, to avoid the embarrassment of failing to fill the quota. Bursa friends called me from Warsaw, urging me to apply, and suggesting that the ministry did not think that I should worry about the past. My credentials fit the requirements well since I spoke Russian. I was accepted, and prepared to travel to Moscow at the beginning of the 1949–50 academic year.

A few hours after arriving in Moscow I went with a group of students for a little sightseeing. We went to Red Square, the Bolshoi Theater, and other famous places. At one point we had to take a bus but did not have any coins for the tickets. A Russian girl noticed our predicament and before we disembarked in disappointment offered to pay for our tickets. It was a very pleasant welcome to the city. We asked for her name and address to return her money, but she refused with a smile.

The next day I began to look for the appropriate university to apply. There were no printed catalogs for the various universities; instead one had to look at billboards on the streets to figure out the programs offered by the various institutions. I was interested in finding a school with a curriculum that emphasized applied subjects as opposed to strictly theoretical courses. I chose the Moscow State Economic Institute, located in a former Russian Orthodox Church at 41 Zatsepa Street. The institute offered courses in macroeconomic planning, economics of enterprises (business economics), accounting, technology of industries, economic geography, national economic planning, among others. However, in every institution, courses in Marxist philosophy, the history of the Bolshevik Party, and Marxist political economy were required. I regarded my choice of school as very fortunate, as on the first day of classes I met Lena Bogolepova—the girl who had paid our fares on the bus. We began a friendship that would endure for a long time, far beyond graduation in 1954.

Russian students didn't avoid mingling with the foreign students, since we all came from friendly countries, the so-called "peoples" democracies. However, most Russian female students were reluctant to get involved with foreign males, as marriage to them was not permitted. Lena took a risk and fell in love with Stojan, a Bulgarian student, and they brought a beautiful baby into the world. The other students were sympathetic and happy for the couple. Lena was not reprimanded, nor was Stojan. The Bulgarian authorities could have sent Stojan home, but they didn't. The mixed couple graduated, the baby thrived, and I saw them again later several times either in Moscow or Sofia.

I spent five years in Moscow, graduating in the highest rank, the equivalent of cum laude in American universities. During those years, I learned a lot about the workings of the Soviet system and about the Russian people. Some of my teachers were very good, others, especially those teaching social sciences, had to follow the Communist Party line strictly, or at least not deviate from it much. Only Stalin could change the curriculum, and he did so a few times, once in linguistics and another time in the Political Economy of Socialism. After he issued a booklet on the latter subject, Stalin caused a complete reversal of the theoretical treatment of many topics. Professor Soloviev, who was teaching the Political Economy of Socialism course at the institute, announced one day that everything we had learned had to be revised. The regime's supreme dictator had absolute power, not only over political, economic, and social issues, but over scientific subjects as well. In all spheres the dictator's word was final.

Well, not exactly! I attended a session at the Economic Institute on the subject of Stalin's scientific discoveries in political economy. A very heated debate ensued between two clearly defined factions. One, represented by the philosopher Zhudin, maintained that Stalin's work raised the level of economic and philosophic sciences to new heights, and the other group, led by the courageous agrarian economist Solertinskaya, suggested that many, if not all, of

Stalin's scientific discoveries were not completely new. Stalin, she maintained, had stated similar views before in his writings and speeches. It was only a matter of proper reading and interpretation to realize that those prior statements explicitly or implicitly led to his current position. Here the chairman, Professor Zhudin, suddenly burst out that "this means that Solertinskaya cannot accept the obvious, that Stalin has reached new, lofty heights of scientific formulation. She is trying to diminish his great achievements." Solertinskaya did not buckle under his attack; she continued to defend her view. I do not know how isolated that incident was, but it revealed that even under the dictatorship there were still honest scholars. Many open discussions on less controversial subjects took place in our institute, which made it a fine school under the circumstances.

Sometime in 1952 Adam Kruczkowski, a leading member of the Polish United Workers Party (PUWP), approached me to ask about my membership in *Cukunft,* the youth organization of the Bund. In the independent Poland after WWI the Bund was one of the strongest political parties among the Jewish population, similar to the Polish Socialist Party. It advocated joining the struggle of the Polish workers and strongly opposed all Zionist groups. In the Soviet Union, after the Bolshevik Revolution, there was a split in the ranks of the Bund. One faction advocated joining the Communist Party, while others preferred to remain independent. Henryk Ehrlich and Victor Alter, both leaders of the Polish Bund, fled the Germans in 1939 to the Soviet Union, where they were arrested and then executed. Under Stalin's regime many members of the Bund were sent to the Gulag or murdered outright. Did Kruczkowski consider me a suitable candidate for punishment? I did not know initially what his intentions were. He urged me to join the PUWP, but only after acknowledging my political mistake. I did not believe there was anything wrong with the *Cukunft*. We had many conversations on that subject, and Kruczkowski continued to press me to join the PUWP. Continued resistance on my part could have meant the end of my education and quite a difficult future in Communist Poland.

May Day and the anniversary of the Bolshevik Revolution (November 7 under the new calendar) were special occasions. They were the only two days when Soviet people were allowed to rally on the streets. These were not spontaneous demonstrations as we know them. Nevertheless, most people enjoyed themselves and even danced in the streets. Also in preparation for those holidays, food supplies improved throughout the country, even in Moscow, where most of the time it was sufficient. For example, in Moscow citrus fruits became available during the holidays.

The demonstrations began with assembly early in the morning in the workplace and in schools. Since May 1 and November 7 were not usually warm days in Moscow, we were cold before we started moving toward the city center (Red Square and the Kremlin wall), where the party bosses reviewed the parade. We tried to keep ourselves warm by having a few drinks before leaving home and then by dancing to the music of a *garmoshka* (accordion) and the singing of a chorus of participants and bystanders.

The parades moved very slowly, especially in the first few hours, when huge columns were directed toward the main city arteries leading to Red Square and the Kremlin. Participants were given banners and slogans to carry and were met by loudspeakers playing music and repeating official slogans approved by the Central Committee of the Communist Party. Occasionally, specific greetings were shouted, for example, when the workers of a favored group entered the square. When students arrived, the announcer praised the *Komsomol* (a Communist youth group) and the Soviet youth for being in the vanguard of the struggle for peace and for preparing themselves to become the instruments of the development of the Fatherland.

The most exciting moment came when our column finally marched into Red Square. We wondered, "Will he be there or not? Will we finally see him?" Of course, we meant Stalin. Usually when we entered Red Square, he wasn't there. Since our institute was located in the Moskvoretsky District, we were placed very close to the Kremlin wall and the Lenin Mausoleum. We would enter Red Square at least three hours after the start of the parade, which always came after the military marched past. By that time, Stalin had tired of watching and listening to all the noise and probably went off for a snack and a little rest inside the Kremlin. However, he would reappear later on. That's why we never knew whether we would see him or not. And seeing him was considered a very big deal.

In the May Day parade of 1952, we entered Red Square about 2:00 P.M. The columns were moving reasonably fast, and we heard the traditional slogans as we approached the Lenin Mausoleum, where, on its balcony, the dignitaries greeted the parade. Then everything suddenly stopped. There was an enormous roar. Looking toward the Lenin Mausoleum, we saw Stalin walking down the steps leading to an underground entry into the Kremlin. He stopped at the foot of the staircase to greet us. He looked shorter than we imagined from pictures. The crowd went wild. Never in my life have I seen such a wild, ecstatic sea of people, screaming, yelling, and falling into one another's arms, jumping for joy. The foreign students, in particular, expressed extreme happiness. They had finally seen him after all those years of disappointment, just like in the pictures (although maybe not as tall), "the leader of all nations, master of all sciences, Father of the Soviet people, the great and beloved Stalin." I can't say that I didn't share in the enthusiasm of the moment to some degree.

But I wasn't dancing and screaming. Rather I watched what went on around me and put it into my memory. For some reason, I stored away a picture of Valtr Komarek, a Czech student who was overjoyed—and who later, during the Velvet Revolution in Czechoslovakia in 1989–90, played a leading role and who was even deputy prime minister for a while. Usually, Valtr was calm, very slow, and not easily excited. We lived in the same dormitory, so we saw each other almost daily. Here in Red Square he was jumping and screaming and falling in the arms of fellow Czech students. And he was not the only one so excited.

Didn't people know what kind of beast in human skin Stalin really was? Didn't they know how many millions died because of him, how many millions were murdered or perished in the Soviet gulags? At that time, especially among students, there was no mention of such matters, for the obvious reason of fearing to become an additional victim of Stalin's regime. Did they not know of his crimes, and, if they did, what were they feeling deep in their hearts? I think not all students knew; the majority believed the propaganda and sincerely admired their leader.

On January 13, 1953, the Communist Party newspaper, *Pravda*, featured a story on the now-infamous "Doctors' Plot." Prominent Jewish doctors were accused of deliberately misdiagnosing Stalin's health problems and applying improper treatment. In the light of the history of Stalin's terror and the fantastic stories that accused his closest comrades, party leaders, and famous military commanders, and even the KGB chairmen themselves of disloyalty and plotting, this newest revelation did not seem outrageous. In those days, many people, especially the young, didn't know or remember the show trials of the 1930s, hence the accusations against the physicians seemed credible.

The shock was enormous, especially among our medical school students, whose top professors were among the accused. Shock and disbelief—this is some terrible mistake! Imagine those respected doctors and academicians deliberately trying to cause Stalin's death! Many of them were accused of being in collusion with and acting on behalf of Zionists and foreign enemies. And it so happened that all those involved were Jewish. What a plot and what an incitement to anti-Semitic prejudice and even pogroms! And all this was supposedly discovered by an obscure physician who was not even close to the Kremlin doctors. How could people believe this? Many did not. It was too much.

According to the historians Jonathan Brent and Vladimir Naumov, the plot was designed to bring about a vast purge of Jews in all institutions, stigmatizing Jews as agents of American-English espionage. The plot implied a larger problem, an American-English espionage system so dangerous and powerful that reaction to it could lead to another international conflict, possibly even nuclear war. I am not sure that I can accept all those far-reaching suppositions of the plot's impact on international affairs, but certainly for the Jews in the Soviet Union it was a very dangerous development, and perhaps for the Jews in other Communist countries as well.

Then, on March 5, 1953, Stalin died. Apparently he was afraid to take medication and to be seen by doctors for fear of being poisoned. Whether true or false, he didn't have proper care after he had a stroke. That's how Beria arranged that it would happen. A complicated game was being played out by Beria, who thought that this time he was going to move faster than Stalin, and would not be his victim, as so many KGB bosses before him had been. In order to avoid the fate of his predecessors, Beria planned to get rid of Stalin first. And he succeeded. Soon after Stalin's death, the story about the doctors was called a complete fabrication in an official statement in *Pravda* on April 6, 1953, and the doctors were immediately rehabilitated. Hadn't Beria prepared the whole story in the first place?

The news of Stalin's death was a shock to the public. His grandeur may have led people to think that he was also immortal. And, suddenly, at a not-very-old age, he died. I was in a factory in Moscow on a class assignment. Each time a statement was read about Stalin's medical condition, everyone ran to the radio. When they broadcast news of his death, people openly wept. At our institute a memorial service was held in the large auditorium, specially decorated for the occasion. Speaker after speaker, some very distinguished professors, could not suppress their anguish and broke down in the middle of their praise and sorrow. Obviously this was contagious. It looked like people sincerely grieved over the loss of their beloved leader. They wondered how and by whom the country would be governed, whether the country would be able to find a leader of Stalin's quality. This was on the surface. What people really thought is anybody's guess.

Stalin's body lay in state in the most prestigious place in Moscow, the *Colonny Zal Doma Sojuzov* (Columned Hall of the House of Unions). In the same hall, the infamous show trials of leaders of the party and the military in the late 1930s had taken place. Millions of people tried to pay their respects. Not all could be accommodated. People were trampled in many places; some were seriously hurt or killed.

A group of Polish students, including myself, tried to get to the site, located in the center of the city at the corner of Gorki and Manezh streets. During those days, all approaches to the place were blocked. Only those with special permits were allowed to enter the hall. Nevertheless, we tried to get through. We got off at the Mayakovski subway station and continued on foot along Gorki Street toward the House of Unions. We tried to pass the roadblocks by showing our foreign passports, adding a few additional words, such as we were a delegation of Polish students coming to pay respect to Comrade Stalin; this seemed to work and we were let through. The closer we got, the more frequent the checkpoints and barriers. Finally, we were allowed to join a line along the sidewalk leading to the building. We moved slowly and in silence until we finally entered the Columned Hall. There were mountains of flowers surrounding Stalin's bier. Several orchestras played sad music, and many dignitaries and official delegations formed an honor guard around the bier. The guard was changed often. We approached Stalin's bier and paid respect. The atmosphere was very subdued and to a degree surreal. It was difficult to realize this absolute ruler was now dead and could not do anything. Was that good or bad? We didn't know.

The troika that took over the government intrigued many of us: Gregory Malenkov (more or less expected), Nikita Khrushchev (not clear), and Beria (ominous). Malenkov's pronouncements at and following the funeral were somewhat encouraging. The Soviet people didn't have to wait long to hear about impending changes. Malenkov stressed economic issues, the standard of living and consumer goods. Rumors reached the academic community about serious disputes on theoretical issues with revisionist undertones. Not long thereafter, the Beria affair developed, bringing more unreal, unbelievable accusations in the old tradition of accusing him of being a spy working for the British and other foreign intelligence agencies since the 1920s! As incredible as those accusations were, the fact that Beria was removed from power was welcome news.

Rumors about revisionist tendencies in the leadership must have been true, since, in a few years, Khrushchev, who soon became the party leader, denounced Stalinism in his famous secret speech to the XX Congress of the Communist Party in March 1956. But this is getting ahead of the story. In the meantime, political prisoners started coming home. Even before that, Efim Voroshilov, who became the country's president (chairman of the Supreme Soviet), declared amnesty for criminal prisoners. As a result, many criminals returned to Moscow and other cities and immediately started terrorizing people, unceremoniously robbing and assaulting the innocent even in public view. It took many months to rid the city of the menace. It was never clear why hard-core criminals were judged worthy of amnesty in the first place.

Life in Moscow was not only study, as I also took advantage of the many cultural and other attractions offered. Foremost was the Bolshoi Theater, with its operas and ballets. MCHAT, the leading theater, and other highly regarded theaters were always a source of cultural riches. Art museums in Moscow were wonderful places to learn about and appreciate world-famous artists and their masterpieces. The Polish embassy was the meeting place for students and our own cultural showcase. We had a choir, a dance troupe, poetry readings, and musical performances. We also put on productions for international student festivals. The embassy was also the place for our political meetings and, from time to time, lavish banquets were given on national holidays (both Polish and Soviet). We enjoyed those parties for their excellent and plentiful food and drink.

The food supply in Moscow was remarkably abundant and of good quality. A variety of smoked fish was a delight to gourmets. There was plenty of inexpensive red and black caviar. Frequently, Jerzy Zachariasz, my roommate, and I had lunch on a quarter pound of red caviar, which cost four rubles. From our monthly stipend of eight hundred rubles we could buy fifty pounds of red caviar. Sausages and cold meats were available in many stores, as were dairy products, especially hard cheeses. When we cooked our own dinner in the dormitory, one favorite was the *sibirskie pelmeni* (meat in pastry shells). We could afford to have dinner in *stolovayas* (restaurants). Our preferred dish was a Caucasian specialty made of lamb. From the same origin was *shashlik* (slices of mutton, broiled on a spit). Chicken kiev was on the menu of the more expensive restaurants, but worth the price. Everywhere one could get the traditional *shci sviezhyje* (fresh cabbage soup) and a variant based on sauerkraut. But the best and most pleasing to me was the *soliyanka*, a very rich soup of cabbage and meat, with slices of sausage and spices. This soup was best on the Moscow-Berlin train, on which I traveled home for vacation. The trips on that train were remarkable for the presence of military officers. I have never seen Soviet officers so relaxed and happy. They returned home for vacation from long service in units stationed in Germany or in southwest Poland. They had money, and most of the time they invited me to join in their celebration. There I learned the joke about ordering vodka: "A Soviet officer in a restaurant is considering how much vodka he should order. One hundred grams might be too little, and 200 grams too much. Okay, he decided, I will order 150 grams twice."

In the spring of 1954, we got the exciting news that the Polish students would be given a tour of the Kremlin. This was extraordinary news, for we never dreamed of being able to see the interior of this famous place. The Kremlin was the Forbidden City that no ordinary person could visit, and now it would be open to us! Certainly it was a sign of the changes that were taking place after Stalin's death. We were among the first foreign student groups given a tour of the entire Kremlin. As we passed through the gate of this grandiose, magnificent place, a panorama of fabulously domed churches appeared before our eyes. Only the highest domes could be seen from outside. We visited the *Uspenski Sobor* (Cathedral of the Dormition), which was built in the second half of the fifteenth century by the Italian architect Fioravanti. Next we saw the *Blagovieshcenski Sobor* (the Cathedral of the Annunciation), built at the same time by Russian masters, and the *Archangelski Sobor* (Cathedral of the Archangel), erected in the beginning of the sixteenth century by Italian architects. Over time, the cathedrals were enlarged, reaching the magnificent form we can observe today. These places of worship were not ones ordinary Russians could attend. They were erected for the Russian rulers, their families, and honored guests. They were essentially museums: richly ornamented, full of masterpieces by the best foreign and Russian artists and exquisite interiors filled with gold and gems.

In the Great Kremlin Palace we admired the magnificent Hall of St. George and the huge hall where the Supreme Soviet and the Central Committee of the Communist Party held their meetings. A year earlier, it was forbidden to take a photograph of the Kremlin. Even now, not all visitors were shown the biggest treasure of the Kremlin, the State Armory. Let this name not mislead anybody. Many centuries ago, it was a place where the best Russian artisans produced arms. Over time, it was transformed into a repository of precious artifacts that arrived as royal gifts from countries throughout the world. It became the richest museum of applied art in the world, as well as including an enormous collection of Russian art. Our student excursion to the Kremlin included a visit to a hall where there was an exhibit of gifts received by Stalin on his seventieth birthday. One quite impressive example stuck in my mind: a gift from Mao Zedong, a tiny, cylinder-like ball made of ivory, about two inches in diameter, inside of which a congratulatory message was engraved. It was so tiny that one could read it only with a magnifying glass. The precision of the Chinese artist's work was wonderful. This visit to the Kremlin was the highlight of my five years in Moscow.

I was surprised at the sight of all these treasures, knowing how poor the Russian people were. More important, I wondered how these treasures, many with religious content, and all those cathedrals had been preserved so well, despite the many upheavals, revolutions, wars, and atheistic Communist rule. The magnificent cathedrals surprised me most. According to legends, there were forty times forty, meaning sixteen hundred churches in Moscow, most of them now closed, converted into movie theaters or storage buildings. There appears to be continuity in the recognition by Kremlin rulers, irrespective of political opinion, that the Kremlin and its rich cathedrals reflect the might of the Russian state.

Moscow was also generous to me on a personal level, for I found my future wife there. A small group of Soviet students at the institute distinguished themselves from the rest, both by age and maturity. These were students who had worked during the war and were therefore late in graduating from high school. They experienced many hardships during the war, and they had personally contributed to victory. Among those was Zina, my future wife. Initially, we didn't think about marriage, because that was forbidden between Soviet and foreign citizens. We enjoyed each other's company and didn't think far ahead. But after Stalin's death, the law was changed. In February 1954 we were married. The ceremony was extremely simple. We applied to the district office of the vital statistics bureau for a marriage certificate. The office was not different from any other office in the Soviet Union: a few desks cluttered with papers, an inkholder, and a nib-pen. The official, a young woman, checked our identity cards, asked a few questions, and put the necessary information into a ledger. After that, she typed the certificate of marriage, pronounced us husband and wife, and we were free to go. There were two witnesses to this ceremony: Nina and Jerzy Zachariasz.

While waiting for our turn to enter the marriage office, we noticed an elderly couple watching us and smiling. "Look," the elderly man said, "I am now marrying my wife for the second time. I married her many years ago, when you weren't even born. After a few years I divorced her, but she did not know it until recently, when we needed our marriage certificate, which I had to turn back in when I divorced her. The law then allowed either one of a married couple to divorce the other by making a statement in an office similar to the one we are in now. In our case, it so happened that we had an argument one morning. I was mad and went out right to the divorce office. In the afternoon, my anger was gone, and I went home, I didn't tell my wife that we were divorced. We lived that way for another thirty years." The bride and groom smiled during this story, and we joined them in laughter.

Within a few months of our wedding, both Zina and I graduated with distinction. Before leaving the Soviet Union, we Polish students went on a tour of the southern part of the USSR, including Rostov, the Ukraine (Kiev, Odessa, and the Crimea), Georgia (Tbilisi, Sukhumi, and Batumi), Azerbaijan, and Armenia. It was a most interesting tour, during which we learned about the people and marveled at the beauty of those places. A particularly interesting part of the trip was the ride from Odessa to Georgia in a luxurious, air-conditioned (a first for me) liner, which belonged to Hitler until 1945. The Soviets took it as part of war reparations and used it as a cruise ship in the Black Sea.

Our Polish colleague Hanka had married Koka, a fellow student from Georgia. During our trip, we visited his parents' house in Batumi. They prepared a lavish party for the entire group. According to Georgian tradition, the head of the household starts with a toast on some pleasant and interesting subject. Each participant around the table adds something on the same subject in subsequent toasts. Since there were about thirty people, many toasts were made and much wine was consumed, which is also a tradition in this land of fine wines.

After my return from this wonderful trip, I had to pack everything and go back to Poland. Zina had not yet gotten the necessary travel documents, but I could no longer stay in the Soviet Union. The time for separation arrived. It was not pleasant, but we were hopeful that everything would work out. I returned to Warsaw a married man, but without my wife.

21

Revolt against Stalinist Excesses in Poland

After Stalin's death, the political situation in Poland started to destabilize, following similar events in the Soviet Union. Beria, the head of the Soviet KGB, was accused of treason, including espionage, and was sentenced to death and executed in December 1955. Then in the spring of 1956 Khrushchev, in a secret speech to the XX Congress of the Communist Party in the Soviet Union, admitted enormous atrocities were committed under Stalin's orders. Poland's president Boleslaw Bierut did not return to Poland from the Moscow Congress. Many suspected that his sudden death involved foul play.

During the summer of 1956, a deep crisis developed in the Polish leadership as popular discontent with governmental policies reached the boiling point. Those advocating more liberal economic and political policies clashed with the old Stalinist leaders of the Polish United Workers Party (Communists). Party leader Edward Ochab, who had replaced Bierut, and others were seeking to restore the imprisoned Wladyslaw Gomulka to power. Socialist university students actively demanded change. In the summer of 1956 factory workers in Poznan went on strike for reforms, and its bloody suppression angered people all over the country. The economic situation was grim and the standard of living had declined; this was not the prosperity promised by implementation of the Six-Year Plan (1949–55). Atrocities perpetuated by the secret police became known and troubled the public. Unrest was in the air.

The Party Committee in the PKPG (State Commission of Economic Planning), where I had found work, decided to address abuses in the agency itself. A report was to be prepared reviewing what had transpired during the Stalinist regime and making recommendations for change. The first draft of the paper was rejected because it didn't go far enough. I was assigned to prepare

a second draft. Thereby I got involved in the heated debate on political liberalization that led to the events of October 1956.

That summer, Poland went through a few months of extreme tension. On
one hand, society, including the United Workers Party, was ready for funda-
mental changes, albeit for the latter still within the confines of a Socialist system. On the other hand, the Soviet Union feared such movements in Poland
and Hungary could get out of control, endangering its hegemony. Moscow
was therefore prepared to suppress any developments that might undermine
their control of Eastern Europe. In the fall of 1956 Nikita Khrushchev and
several top officials of the Soviet Communist Party suddenly showed up in
Warsaw; there were movements of Soviet military units toward that city. One
day I happened to visit the *Sejm*, the Polish Parliament, and witness an in-
quiry by Boleslaw Drobner (formerly a member of the Polish Socialist Party)
addressed to Prime Minister Jozef Cyrankiewicz, questioning the movement
of Soviet troops in Polish territory. Cyrankiewicz admitted that such movements were indeed under way, but expressed confidence that issues would be
resolved peacefully. The Polish leadership persuaded Khrushchev that developments in Poland presented no danger to the Soviet Union. The situation in
Hungary was more critical and dangerous. The Stalinist regime in Hungary
was more harsh than in Poland and, encouraged by events in Warsaw, de-
mands for reform there went much further, including, at the height of the
revolt, a demand that Hungary leave the Warsaw Pact. A Hungarian uprising
ended tragically with bloody intervention by the Soviet army.

A pithy and accurate description of the atmosphere among the nonparti-
san intelligentsia in Poland was made by one of my office colleagues: "Let's
open the window and scream: 'Under the leadership of the Soviet Union! (*Ze
Zwiazkiem Radzieckim na czele!*)'" This would reassure Moscow and cover all
proposals, no matter how extreme, and such a slogan was indeed used in Polish Party propaganda.

By the end of October, the long-expected change in the party leadership
finally occurred. During a special meeting of the Polish United Workers Party
Central Committee lasting several days, there was a general summons to
party cells throughout the country. Along with the clear desire by a large part
of the party to retain Socialist direction of the country's development, there
was fear that the tide of reform might move too far to the right. The center
of the reform movement, certainly with its most uncompromising advocates,
was in the Warsaw Polytechnic. Thousands of students rallied day and night

as the Central Committee meeting was taking place. Revolutionary fervor was contagious, and I could not resist the desire to enter the Polytechnic to see what was going on. I had a close association with Polytechnic students, as I had been teaching political economy there for the previous two years. Students blocked the entry to the building, but through back doors I found a way to reach the place where the students were meeting. The central part of the Polytechnic building is a rotunda, with balconies from floor to ceiling leading to classrooms on four or five levels. The student rally was on the first floor, but people jammed the balconies on each level. Their raucous shouts of approval or disapproval echoed so loudly that it was impossible for me to stand it for more than a few minutes. And yet most students had been there for days. When I arrived, they were playing a tape of the Central Committee speech of the ZMP leader Helena Jaworska, which was received with great enthusiasm.

I remember a phrase that represents the mood of the students and their cause. It was in a satirical sketch put on by the student theater: "And shit attached itself to the boat of the Socialist revolution and is calling, sail on!" The students wanted the revolution cleansed of its impurities.

There was joy in the hope that Poland could now manage its affairs in a more humane way, with a greater degree of independence. By the end of October 1956, Wladyslaw Gomulka became first secretary of the party and essentially head of the government. At the end of the stormy session of the Party Central Committee, he gave a rousing speech condemning the Stalinist regime in blunt terms, and promised a more liberal and independent policy. He called a rally at the plaza near the *Palac Kultury* (a high-rise building, ostensibly a gift from Stalin to the Polish nation), attended by more than 300,000 enthusiastic listeners. He summarized the events leading to his return to power and, at the end, called for an end to rallies and a return to work.

Judging from the situation in the Planning Commission (PKPG), a large number of activists were immersed in political debates and meetings. After one such meeting with the chairman of the PKPG, Deputy Prime Minister Eugeniusz Szyr, which lasted until 3:00 A.M., I chanced to get a ride home in the chairman's car. Conversation with him centered on the question, was it true that people were not working? It was true indeed, and was apparently so widespread that Gomulka had to appeal to the nation to go back to work.

After Gomulka's rally, there was a small demonstration in front of the Soviet embassy. I went over to watch a small and peaceful gathering of young people. It was entirely spontaneous and after a while the participants dispersed. The boulevard where the Soviet embassy was had been renamed Stalin Boulevard a few years earlier, but had regained its original name Aleje Ujazdowskie. During the German occupation it was Adolf Hitler Strasse. Some other names of cities and streets were also changed. The industrial center of the Silesian region, Katowice, had been renamed Stalinogrod a few years earlier. It got its old name back.

A final celebration took place a few weeks later, when Gomulka went to Moscow as the head of a Polish delegation. During a farewell rally in Warsaw, and later in each place his train stopped, people gathered and sang *"Sto Lat,"* which ordinarily is sung at birthday parties. This time the song acquired a political meaning, wishing Gomulka "100 years." I am sure that many people later regretted their good wishes, but at the time those feelings were spontaneous. The message was clear: be firm in negotiating with the Soviets. One of the many issues that Poles resented was the low price paid for Polish coal sent to the Soviet Union.

In mid-1955, one of Poland's well-known economist, Professor Michal Kalecki, had been invited to return to the country. We knew very little about him, although he was an early proponent of the Keynesian economic theory that revolutionized policy throughout the world. I don't recall that his name and contributions to economic theory were ever mentioned during my student years in Moscow. I surmise that he was as little known to students in Poland. Kalecki began as a student in the Gdansk Polytechnic and then turned to economics. He left Poland before the war, thereby avoiding the fate of many Jewish victims of the Nazis. During the war he worked at the Oxford University Institute of Statistics, where he concentrated on the war economy. He made outstanding contributions to the analysis of the dynamics of capitalist and socialist economies. After the war, he headed the Industrial Department of the Secretariat of the United Nations, where he was charged with preparing the World Economic Reports. In 1955 Deputy Prime Minister Hilary Minc invited Kalecki to return to Poland. Minc was responsible for economic development and appointed Kalecki as his chief economic advisor.

I met Kalecki in early 1956 at a lecture he gave to Planning Commission employees. It was truly an extraordinary lecture. He was very precise. He used mathematical formulae to develop his argument and demonstrate his points. At the conclusion of the talk Kalecki got a standing ovation, not often conferred on an economist. In 1958 Kalecki assembled a team of experts to formulate a projection for a Fifteen-Year Plan for economic development in Poland. I was invited to join the team and was charged with the part of the plan dealing with demand for labor and productivity in all sectors of the economy.

The next ten years of Poland's history were a mixture of some improvements in the standard of living and the political climate, but those advancements were reversed in the early 1960s. Alas, Gomulka soon forgot his promises and went back to dictatorial methods.

22
Mobilization of Reserve Officers in 1967

In the summer of 1967, the military authorities ordered a wide mobilization of reservists. I was assigned to the reserves when I left the army nearly twenty years before, and by this time I had been promoted to the rank of lieutenant. I was ordered to report to the Warsaw air base in Okecie. Since graduating from the university, I had managed to avoid being called up; this was a benefit available to employees of the Planning Commission, of which I was glad to take advantage. The general who was the head of the military department in the Planning Commission was kind enough to write to the regional military headquarters, asking that I be deferred because I was working on an important assignment that could not be postponed. I used that excuse several times. But in 1967, no such pleas were accepted, as the situation was very tense.

The Six Days' War between Israel and the Arab countries broke out June 5, 1967, with the invasion of Israel by Egypt, Jordan, and Syria. Iraq, Kuwait, Saudi Arabia, Sudan, and Algeria declared war in their support. The war followed the blockade by Egypt of the Tiran Straits, which closed the international waterway through the Gulf of Aqaba to Israeli shipping. On May 16, 1967, President Gamal Abdel Nasser of Egypt ordered that UN Emergency Forces on the Egyptian-Israeli border be withdrawn. Arab countries called for a war of total annihilation against Israel. For its success in the war, Israel took from Egypt the Sinai Desert and the Gaza Strip; from Jordan, the eastern side of Jerusalem and the West Bank; and from Syria, the Golan Heights.

The Soviet Union's position was clear: full support for the Arab countries. Poland initially took a somewhat ambiguous position, not exactly in tune with the USSR. Poland's president Ochab made a somewhat less bellicose statement than the other Warsaw Pact countries. That independent thinking was soon rectified. On June 9, 1967, Warsaw Pact nations meeting in Moscow decided to break diplomatic relations with Israel (only Romania did not follow that decision). Within a week, the Israeli ambassador to Poland left the country to the music of a chorus of some two hundred drunken Poles, who were brought to the airport by the secret police for that purpose.

On active duty I could observe the mood and sympathies of an important part of the officer corps of the Polish Army. I served at an air base near Warsaw and commuted by truck every day with other officers. Initially they were very happy to hear the claims of the Egyptians about the many Israeli planes they had shot down. Their mood changed after hearing the next day that the Israelis had destroyed a lot of Egyptian planes, not the other way around. Still, the next day, I heard stories repeated that "German SS officers were commanding the Israeli army." What a bizarre propaganda invention, to link Israel with Nazism! Then the tone changed to stories about how well equipped the Israeli soldier was. "Imagine," they said, "each one of them has a radio." And finally, on the fifth or sixth day, the officers were saying, "We were told that Jews didn't know how to fight. What a lie."

The base political commissar assembled all the officers one day, and in a speech made the following attempt at irony: "We are behaving like Christians; when you get hit on one cheek, turn the other cheek." The mood was clearly anti-Israeli. There was disappointment with Arab failures and the outcome of the war. There was also an assumption that mobilization would lead to military intervention by the Warsaw Pact. Maybe they wanted a little adventure to teach the Jews a lesson themselves or to help the Arabs push Israel into the sea. Instead, they realized that after six days the war was over and no intervention would take place.

In case war broke out, my duty was to command the air base repair shop with the rank of major. In the meantime, I sat all day looking out at the runway where the military planes took off. I was given some brochures to read with ridiculous instructions on what to do in case of a nuclear attack by the Americans and other imperialists. I was given a tour of facilities at the base, even being shown where some secret gear was stored.

It was terribly boring, and I asked for a more meaningful assignment. The commander suggested I present a talk on the Polish economic situation to junior officers at the base. I gladly agreed and, one late afternoon, outlined my thoughts to them. I was rather critical of the economic situation, but didn't realize how hostile those junior officers were toward the government. They freely expressed their dissatisfaction with government policy and openly criticized Prime Minister Jozef Cyrankiewicz. In response to that criticism, one officer joked that he knew of no example of a corporal making a successful revolution. After ten days of this, I was demobilized.

The Israeli victory in the Six Days' War had very serious repercussions for the tiny population of Jews still in Poland. The regime, and especially unruly officers in the Polish military, could not accept the Arab defeat. It was humiliating to the USSR and the entire Soviet bloc that had supplied the Arabs with arms, provided military training, and given economic and technical assistance. At the height of the cold war this was intended to establish the USSR as the most influential power in the Middle East, in competition with the West. The Israeli victory was a severe blow.

A few weeks later Wladyslaw Gomulka was upset by rumors that some Jewish newspaper correspondents had celebrated Israel's victory in a publishing office. In a speech to the Trade Union Congress, he lashed out at Zionists and Poles of Jewish origin, calling them a "fifth column," a dangerous accusation in a country far from free of ethnic nationalism and bigotry against the remnant of the Jewish community. The notion of a fifth column, or, as others said, "a state within a state," which equated the few Jews still in high positions to a government apart from the rightful Polish authorities, was ominous. Gomulka also invited Jews to leave the country, if they so desired, since, as he said, "Polish citizens should have only one fatherland." In those days, a joke by the famous novelist Antoni Slonimski circulated in Poland. He said: "I agree with comrade Gomulka that everyone in Poland should have one fatherland, but why should it be Egypt?"

But not only Jews were happy with the outcome of the war. General sympathy was with Israel, for some reason. Perhaps for the surprising brevity of the war and the mettle of Israeli fighters, contrary to the stereotype many Poles still harbored that Jews lacked the valor and discipline to fight effectively. Others saw in this a way to express disapproval of the Soviet Union. A widespread idea emerged that "our Jews beat their Arabs" ("our Jews" reflecting the belief that most Israelis were of Polish origin, while "their Arabs" meant the Soviet client Arabs), which could not be well received by Russians. Also a factor was the simple decency of people who saw the aggression by the Arab countries, especially of Egypt's Nasser. A significant role in shaping these views was played by Cardinal Stefan Wyszynski, who on June 6 at a mass in Warsaw appealed to believers "to pray for the fighting Israelis, whose na-

tion had been condemned to death many times in the past, despite the fact
that it had a right to an independent existence."

Gomulka's charge that Jews represented a fifth column was not endorsed
by the Polish Politburo. President Edward Ochab demanded that this charge
be struck from the published version of the speech. It was the first time censorship was applied to a first secretary of the Communist Party. Nevertheless,
Gomulka had set something in motion that was grasped and effectively used
by the Moczar faction to launch an anti-Zionist (but in fact, anti-Jewish)
campaign. General Mieczyslaw Moczar, a nationalistic officer who held posts
in the Ministry of State Security (the secret police) and the powerful Association of War Combatants and Resistance Fighters, aspired to usurp power
from Gomulka. He had a strong following in the party as well.

It would not be correct to assume that Moczar was waiting for a signal
or that without it, he wouldn't have found another pretext for launching an
attack on Gomulka, using deeply ingrained anti-Semitic bigotry as a convenient vehicle. The Moczar group had infiltrated the party apparatus and the
party cells in most government institutions for quite some time. In the Planning Commission, those in Moczar's group were systematically replacing old-
generation Communists. Moczar's people were held in reserve until the signal
to attack was given.

23
The 1968 Student Revolt in Poland

March 8, 1968, was to be an important date in my education. I was on my way to Warsaw University to sign up for the Ph.D. program. The program required that I pass two exams: political economy and Marxist philosophy. The most important task was the presentation of a doctoral dissertation and its defense at a public session with the appropriate faculty members. To satisfy the requirement of public participation, the proceedings had to be announced in the newspaper and anyone, even from outside the academic community, had a right to be present and ask questions, even if unrelated to the subject.

Despite the tense atmosphere in Warsaw, I didn't expect to be confronted with a situation that completely derailed my plans. It was not only the matter of an advanced degree. I had been in discussions with Professor Jozef Pajestka of Warsaw University about joining the Planning Institute he headed, a prestigious research facility within the Planning Commission. Professor Pajestka had agreed to supervise my dissertation. But events at the university that morning threw all my plans into question.

The entry to the university was blocked by a rally. The protest had started with an incident at the National Theater in Warsaw. In November 1967 its artistic director, Kazimierz Dejmek, staged a play based on the poem *Dziady*, written by Poland's beloved Adam Mickiewicz. The show was received enthusiastically, especially the lines referring to the tsarist Russian despotism, police methods, and stupid bureaucratic machine. Gomulka later was to quote the following lines, spoken by a Russian character, which especially offended him as politically suspect: "No wonder that the Poles curse us. For a century Moscow has sent them our worst scoundrels in droves." The show's lead actor,

Gustav Holoubek, and the entire cast were applauded tumultuously, returning for fifteen curtain calls.

From the time the play opened, party leaders and apparatchiks were unhappy with the show, charging that, instead of its anti-tsarist themes, Dejmek had emphasized anti-Russian aspects, which, according to them, were politically unacceptable. There were rumors that the Soviet ambassador had expressed displeasure and suggested the show be closed. Soviet authorities apparently denied these rumors.

By January 30, 1968, the party had decided to close the play, causing widespread protest by intellectuals and students. A large group of students attended the last show, holding a banner calling for "independence without censorship." At the end of the show, they held a thirty-minute demonstration in the theater and then, joined by many others, went to the Mickiewicz monument on Krakowskie Przedmiescie. There the police arrested many of the participants.

The next day, the press announced the arrest of many students, emphasizing those with Jewish surnames or those known to be of Jewish origin. The students then circulated a petition to the *Sejm* (parliament), protesting the closing of *Dziady* and more generally defending national culture and freedom of expression. Within the first two weeks of February they collected 3,145 signatures in Warsaw and 1,098 in Wroclaw. Irena Lasota delivered the petition to parliament on February 16.

After further attempts to discredit Dejmek, he was expelled from the Communist Party and fired from his position as artistic director of the theater. In a propaganda leaflet spread by the Moczar group, this incident was used to sneer at "Jews who are trying to teach us the values of our national culture."

In mid-February the Warsaw Literary Union called a special session to consider the state of Polish culture in light of the closing of *Dziady*. At the meeting they succeeded in adopting a resolution demanding far-reaching changes in cultural policy, liberalization of censorship, and the return of *Dziady* to the repertoire of the National Theater. Many famous and respected writers criticized the government's cultural policy and censorship. Those voices were in turn opposed by writers supporting government policy. The meeting ended abruptly late at night when it was learned that trucks had arrived filled with "workers" demanding admittance to let the writers know what the working class of Warsaw thought about their speeches. How did these "workers" know what was being said at a meeting that was still in progress and that they weren't attending? Coincidentally, the party members left the meeting a half-hour before the trucks arrived. It was clearly another provocation by the secret police, to manipulate events in their interests.

Provocations continued at the university as well. It became a war of leaflets between the students seeking democratic reforms and a group of anti-Semitic provocateurs seeking a reaction they could exploit. The students decided to hold a mass demonstration to publicize their grievances against the punishment of students who were heavily fined for the demonstration at the Mickiewicz monument, and the university president's recommendation that two student leaders be expelled, Michnik and Szlajfer, both of Jewish origin. The rally was set for noon on March 8, 1968. It was declared illegal by university authorities. At the rally the students approved two resolutions: one prepared by Irena Lasota calling for the freedoms guaranteed by the Polish constitution and for an end to the repression of students who participated in the previous demonstration; and a second expressing support for the decisions of the extraordinary meeting of the Warsaw Literary Union, especially for return of *Dziady* to the repertoire of the National Theater. The rally seemed almost over when the trouble started.

Seven buses marked "excursion" entered campus. The "civilians" or "workers" who stepped off those buses immediately started shoving students, at first gently, but then more forcefully. There was no doubt that those so-called workers or "activists," as the official press later characterized them, were actually policemen. This was evident from the well-organized way in which they acted. Students mocked them as "Gestapo," for the way they looked and behaved. A small group of about two hundred students from the official Socialist Youth Organization openly acted in concert with the "excursionists," pointing out student leaders for beating and later arrest. The police thugs were armed with metal-filled truncheons rather than the usual rubber-filled variety.

The vice president of the university, Zygmunt Rybicki, asked the students to leave within fifteen minutes. At that moment, the dean of the economics department, Professor Czeslaw Bobrowski, arrived on the scene, as a student delegation to Rybicki demanded the departure of the "workers" and the militia who had surrounded the university, and the return of seized student identification cards. Professor Bobrowski, in his dean's robe, circulated among the students, asking them to go home, since the rally had already accomplished its purpose. He then talked to the group from the buses, and they agreed to leave as well. The students were promised that the concentration of militia around the university would be withdrawn. Following Dean Bobrowski, the students started to leave. However, instead of withdrawing, the "workers" returned to the university plaza, assaulting students viciously—not the usual occasional knock of a billy club to disperse demonstrators. They wanted to teach the students a lesson by hitting hard, without mercy. Many eyewitnesses described bullies striking students wildly, even girls, when they were already knocked down. Ironically, this was the day when Communists "celebrate" Women's Day.

The "workers" aimed especially at dark-haired girls, assuming they were Jewish. Even older people, who could easily have been supposed to be faculty members, were not spared. The workers followed the students into university buildings and continued to beat them there. They blocked neighboring streets and attacked everyone there, especially young people, who were not necessarily students. Several militia and special army units, as well as the police thugs, took part in the brutality. It was carefully organized and supervised by the Warsaw Party apparatus, together with the secret police.

By that evening, rumors spread that a pregnant student had been killed. The same rumors, with calls for revenge, were more widely spread the next day. Provocative leaflets were distributed, but clearly they were not written by students. Their purpose was to incite further unrest and justify severe repression against seemingly seditious and mendacious students. The story of the pregnant student who was supposedly killed was also a setup to discredit student accounts of violence, as the student, Maria Baraniecka, dramatically showed up on live TV a few days later.

In the following days, the controlled press described the events of March 8 as excesses by hooligans and unruly students, falsifying everything that had happened. That was the provocation that caused the students to continue their protests. On March 9, students of the Warsaw Polytechnic held a rally inside their school, chanting the soon-popular slogan "the press lies!" At the end of the Polytechnic rally, students formed a column of five thousand that grew to twenty thousand, and proceeded toward the office of the newspaper, *Zycie Warszawy*, which had first published a false account of the March 8 events. The students burned newspapers, calling on the workers and townspeople of Warsaw for support. People on the streets threw flowers at the students, in open sympathy.

The police again met the demonstration with violence. In a new twist, the authorities tried to present the unrest as a problem caused by Jews. Two leaflets disseminated by the government on Sunday, March 10, launched that sinister effort. In the first, entitled, "Who Do You Support?" they made sure that all student leaders they named were Jewish and commented that these were children of the "establishment" who despised workers and peasants. In the second leaflet, they charged that the protests were inspired and organized by Zionists. The intent was clear: the trouble was stirred up by Jews and Zionists, people contemptuous of "real" Poles.

On March 11, a huge rally was held in Warsaw, accompanied by fierce battles between students and the police along Krakowskie Przedmiescie and Nowy Swiat, from the student dorms right up to the front of the Party Central Committee building. Student unrest spread across the country.

Wladyslaw Gomulka, first secretary of the PZPR, called a meeting of Warsaw party activists for March 19. There was a great deal of hope that a leader would defuse the tense and angry situation and respond to the student grievances. The students were to be greatly disappointed. Gomulka lashed out at them, repeating the most inflammatory accusations spread by the official media. Instead of being magnanimous and statesmanlike, he heightened the crisis by also attacking the writers' union over the *Dziady* affair. To students it was evident that the political system responded to their concerns with violence and insult. No dialogue was possible, and the students entered a new, more radical phase of their struggle.

The Warsaw Polytechnic students decided the next day to hold a forty-eight-hour sit-in strike. The previously elected Student Committee became the Strike Committee. The rector declared the strike illegal. To prevent provocateurs and secret police from entering, Polytechnic students established strict rules for admission to the building. Those guarding the entrance to the Polytechnic asked people without student IDs to solve a math problem that every student should know. Obviously, those who failed were not students.

The Warsaw population was in support of the striking students. I saw people near the Polytechnic fences delivering food, cigarettes, flowers, and other items to the students. What was going on inside the school and throughout the entire country we learned from Radio Free Europe, our source of reliable information for many years.

On March 22 Education Minister Henryk Jablonski sent an ultimatum to the striking students at Warsaw Polytechnic ordering them to leave the premises by nine that night. He threatened to shut down the entire school if his order was disobeyed. This threat left the students with no options. Slowly, accompanied by professors, most students left during the night for their dormitories.

A similar strike took place at Warsaw University. After a few days, strength and commitment to continue the struggle weakened. The strike committee, under enormous pressure from university authorities, split into factions. Professor Bobrowski convinced the students to write a letter to Gomulka, pledging commitment to building a Socialist Poland and to the alliance with the Soviet Union, and suggesting a dialogue with the authorities. After several days, a response from Prime Minister Jozef Cyrankiewicz stated that the time for dialogue had passed, and that the government would maintain its policy. The minister of education announced the firing of leading professors in the philosophy and economics departments, including Bronislaw Baczko, Leszek Kolakowski, Stefan Morawski, and Wlodzimierz Brus, all professors of high reputation and respected by the students.

The university students rose again to protest, this time against the decision to fire the professors. On March 28 a student rally at Warsaw University adopted a "Declaration of the Student's Movement," demanding economic reform, an end to censorship, independent labor unions, an independent judiciary, and the creation of a constitutional convention. The declaration was the most politically mature and important result of the student revolt, and it was adopted by the Solidarity movement in the 1980s.

In response to the latest rally, the authorities arrested members of the Student Committee. The rector dissolved the departments of economics and philosophy, ended psychology courses in the education department, and dropped the third year of the mathematics and physics departments, the areas of the university that produced the most committed student activists. As a result, 1,616 students were expelled from the university. The student revolt in Poland came to an end.

The Polish student revolt should be considered one of the finest moments in the history of the Polish nation, not only because of the determination to fight for and defend freedom, but also for the maturity of the movement in withstanding enormous pressure to divert it toward a chauvinistic, anti-Semitic movement. Almost all resolutions adopted by the students at rallies, and slogans chanted at street demonstrations, explicitly rejected the authorities' accusation that Jews were leading them astray. The effort of the government and the Communist Party to enlist the university community in an anti-Jewish campaign misfired. Students saw through the plan and rejected it. The use of thugs to create a schism between students and workers also failed. The meetings organized by the party in most state enterprises that adopted resolutions condemning the students, were expressions of party apparatchiks, not workers. Having lost credibility and support in opposing the student movement, the party, in conjunction with the police apparatus, switched gears to purge the Jewish population still remaining in Poland. The anti-Semitic subtext during the student revolt turned into a fully orchestrated dramatic opera by bigots in Communist costumes.

24
The Purge of Jews

On May 1, 1968, Poland's leading communist newspaper, *Trybuna Ludu,* ran a photo on its front page of a banner at a factory that read: "Zionists to Palestine." This was the same slogan used by the right-wing-extremist National Democrat Party before the war. Saying "Zionists" instead of Jews didn't mislead anyone. So the Communist Party joined the ND under the same banner "Jews to Palestine." The party policy was not new, but I considered the use of that slogan as an official announcement of anti-Semitism for the entire world to see.

The wave of purges started with the firing of leading Jewish professors at Warsaw University and other academic institutions. It then spread to government agencies, always preceded by stormy party meetings, in which accusatory speeches were made, based on material presented by Moczar's secret police. These meetings were held at the end of May and in early June at the Planning Commission by the Council of Ministers (*Komisja Planowania przy Radzie Ministrów,* where I was employed). The meetings lasted three days and were thoroughly scripted. Several department heads in the Planning Commission were Jews. Most of them were longtime party members, some since the prewar years, as was Halina Diamand, head of the Department of Employment and Wages. She served as a deputy commander of a tank battalion in the Kosciuszko Army, and her name was often cited in accounts of the heroic battles of that tank unit. Immediately after the war, Halina was assigned to take over from the Red Army factories on German territories assigned to Poland's new frontiers. Later she was transferred to the Central Planning Commission (CPC), where she became a department head. The specific charges against her were for actions she had taken as secretary of the

CPC's party cell in the early 1950s, a period of severe Stalinist repression in Poland and in all Soviet satellite countries. I am sure she was faithfully implementing directives from party leadership. That period had already been thoroughly reviewed in 1956, and reforms had been made. There was no need to return to those days in 1968. Furthermore, there were many non-Jewish party members who also implemented Stalinist directives, and none of them was accused in 1968 for actions taken in the early 1950s. Clearly, it was a vendetta against Jewish party members.

Only Stefan Jedrychowski, chairman of the Planning Commission, had the courage to characterize the speeches, about forty in all, as right-wing, ND Jew-hater's rhetoric, as heard before the war. But even he sounded apologetic and defensive when it came to personnel. In a few months, Jedrychowski was removed from the chairmanship of the Planning Commission and named minister of foreign affairs. In a statement many years later, Jedrychowski repeated that "he felt as if he were once again at a pre-war ONR [semi-fascist organization] rally."

Halina Diamand was expelled from the party along with Zygmunt Adelis, director of the Department of Internal Trade; Leopold Held, a respected chemical engineer; and Franciszka Oliwa, from the archives. Expulsion from the party was tantamount to losing your job as well. Many more Jews were subsequently fired from the Planning Commission. Among those was my institute classmate and close friend, Jerzy Zachariasz. After our graduation and return from Moscow, we were both assigned to the PKPG in 1954, where we started out in the position of "senior advisors," as did many other graduates. In a short time, Jerzy proposed a radical reform of the price system in Poland. His idea was to base Poland's wholesale prices on world prices. The paper he presented was supported by many experts and, since department director Augustowski was leaving his post, Jerzy was offered the directorship of the Department of Costs and Price Policy. He was one of the youngest directors. His appointment was based on education, ability, and innovative ideas. Professor John Michael Montias of Yale University, who was visiting Poland at that time, later wrote: "In December 1956, Jerzy Zachariasz, who was soon to become director of the Department of Costs and Price Policy, introduced the idea that the relations among prices of raw materials traded by Poland, such as coal, iron ore, nonferrous metals, sulfur, and grain, should be patterned as far as possible after the structure of world prices." Zachariasz implemented his idea after being appointed, and he worked closely with the chairman of the Planning Commission, Stefan Jedrychowski, who was also a member of the Politburo. When the renowned economist Michal Kalecki returned to Poland and joined the Planning Commission, Zachariasz worked closely with him as well.

The stormy party meeting in the ministry of foreign affairs acquired great importance, because Foreign Minister Adam Rapacki (a Politburo member) was opposed to the planned anti-Semitic tenor of the meeting. Rapacki was well known in international circles for his proposal in the middle 1950s to establish a nuclear-free zone in Central Europe. The meeting was of great interest to me, for the role played by Adam Kruczkowski, the deputy minister. He was among those who prepared a list of Jews to be purged from the ministry. And it was that list that infuriated Rapacki, causing him to abruptly resign his post.

I had known Kruczkowski since 1949. Both of us studied in the Moscow Economic Institute during the 1949–54 academic years. For five years we lived in the same dormitory, in rooms two yards apart. Kruczkowski was the leader of the Association of Polish Students in the USSR, and for a few of those years I was also a member of its leadership. I had ample opportunity to learn about his character and political views. Adam was a very capable student, hard working, and always following the party line, eagerly doing what was required of him and often anticipating what he should do, even when not asked. After returning to Poland in 1954, he advanced rapidly in the ministry of foreign affairs, and by 1968 had already been a deputy foreign minister for several years. In that capacity he prepared the list of Jews from the ministry to be purged.

One of the most bizarre cases involved Deputy Minister Marian Naszkowski. I had seen him often when I was a student in Moscow during his tenure as Polish ambassador. Kruczkowski occasionally met with the ambassador as leader of Polish students. Naszkowski was presumed to be Jewish because he was dark haired and had what were considered "Semitic" features. Those who knew Naszkowski considered him a "pure Pole." But even if he was Jewish, such an accusation was in itself a racist expression. The secret police worked very hard to prepare lists of Jews and often made mistakes for which they only rarely apologized. Whatever the truth, preparing such a list in the foreign ministry was against the policy of Minister Rapacki, so Kruczkowski's action was also an act of insubordination.

Another case was that of my old friend Eugene Eisenberg. He was a graduate of the Bauman Institute in Moscow, the equivalent of MIT. Eisenberg won a prestigious prize in Poland as Inventor of the Year for designing a new engine. When Poland and Czechoslovakia decided to cooperate in the design and production of a new tractor, Eisenberg was sent to Czechoslovakia to head a team of Polish engineers, and he remained there and worked for several years. Suddenly in 1968 he was fired. Here, as in so many other cases, accusers could not justify their action by pointing to lack of qualifications for the position held. Pure and simple, the reasons were racist. The Eisenberg family emigrated to the United States, where he was immediately hired by the Mack Truck company to head a team of engine designers. It was a clear loss for Poland and a gain for the United States.

The anti-Jewish campaign produced a schism at the highest level and led to a dramatic response from President Edward Ochab, who resigned from all his party and government posts. In his statement, he said: "As a Pole and Communist, I protest with the deepest indignation the anti-Semitic uproar organized in Poland by various dark forces, by yesterday's ONR members and their powerful protectors. As a result of the situation that has developed in our Party, I am compelled to protest by resigning as a member of the Politburo and Central Committee of the Polish United Workers Party (PZPR). At the same time I am submitting a written resignation from the post of Chairman of the State Council and the Chairman of the All State Front of National Unity." Before making this statement public, Ochab had a meeting with Gomulka in which Prime Minister Jozef Cyrankiewicz and Politburo member Zenon Kliszko were present. One can surmise that Ochab thought that a discussion with the party leadership and his threat of resignation would convince Gomulka to reverse the shameful government course. In a later interview, Ochab described Gomulka as exceptionally calm during the meeting. The only justification Gomulka gave for that anti-Semitic policy was that the international situation was very dangerous. Specifically, he mentioned that serious counterrevolutionary preparations were underway in Czechoslovakia of the type seen in Hungary in 1956. Consider the logic: because there was a freedom movement in Czechoslovakia, Polish communists had to purge their nation's remaining Jews!

The harsh response to the student movement, the false accusations against Jews, and the anti-Semitism of official propaganda were directed against Gomulka's regime. Behind that effort was General Mieczyslaw Moczar, the head of the police and security apparatus. He worked hard for many years to put his followers, many of them from the police, into high positions in various government and party institutions. General Moczar's followers, known as the "partisans," opposed the governing elite that, to a large extent, came from Polish Communists who had survived the war in the Soviet Union. The power struggle reached its climax in 1968. Purging the Jews remaining in leading positions was part of that movement (few Jews survived who had not been in the Soviet Union), while anti-Semitic rhetoric was the vehicle to attract mass support to Moczar. Propaganda went so far as to claim that Zionists were planning to seize power in a coup d'etat. Gomulka could not stem that process and, in many ways, was fostering it. He seemed paralyzed by fear of the developing "Prague Spring" in Czechoslovakia.

In the beginning of 1968 Alexander Dubcek replaced Novotny as the Czech party leader. He embarked on a course to create what he called "Socialism with a human face." Censorship was abolished, political freedoms flourished; there was even talk of allowing opposition parties. Czech economist Otto Sik introduced economic reforms that, to a large extent, did away with the Soviet model of central planning, allowing elements of a market economy to take hold.

In the eyes of the Soviets and Polish and East German leaders, the Czech experiments undermined their totalitarian structures and could spread the "freedom virus" to their countries. Gomulka was very active in planning with his counterpart in East Germany for military intervention in Czechoslovakia. An invasion of Czechoslovakia by the Warsaw Pact countries, including Poland and Germany, would remind the Czechs of their loss of the Sudetenland to Nazi Germany in 1939, and of Zaolzie, a small region in northern Czechoslovakia, to Poland. Even such an association with the shameful past did not prevent Gomulka from offering the Polish Army as part of the invasion of Czechoslovakia. The leading force in that adventure was, of course, the Soviet army. On August 21 a joint force from the Soviet Union, Poland, East Germany, Bulgaria, and Hungary invaded Czechoslovakia. Dubcek's experiment with Socialism was brutally crushed.

After losing control of the party apparatus and the propaganda machine, Gomulka vainly tried to counterattack the excesses of Moczar's group. He pointed out the falsity of a few of their accusations, forbade the use of "Zionism" as an epithet, and appealed for a stop to government intrigue. It did not stop.

25
Exodus from Poland

At the meeting in the Planning Commission I was not attacked personally, but that didn't mean I could pretend that nothing was happening. Comecon is the name used in the West for the Council of Mutual Economic Assistance (CMEA), of which most Communist countries were members. I was part of the group of experts, the Comecon Productivity Group, that compared labor productivity in Comecon countries, and I headed the Polish delegation to its meetings. In the beginning of 1967 the administration hired a fellow who had no knowledge of the subject to accompany me to the meetings. I realized that he was from the secret police, and I was very careful about what I said.

At some point in 1968 there were rumors that I was to be named deputy director of the Department of Labor and Wages when a vacancy occurred. I believed that this was part of the propaganda to demonstrate that another Jew was after a high position in the government. Over the fourteen years I worked in the Planning Commission my attitude was not to make myself available for higher positions, precisely in order to avoid such accusations. All that time I remained at my starting rank of senior advisor. Many people with less education and experience advanced to higher positions. I worked hard, applied my knowledge to the task at hand, and was very successful, but avoided promotion. In the summer of 1968 I was not sent to a Comecon study group meeting in Bulgaria. Instead, the new fellow headed the Polish delegates. That was a clear indication that I was considered untrustworthy. My first response was to return my party membership card. My visit to the party secretary was not pleasant, even though he tried to convince me that the anti-Semitic policy would end some day.

After much painful analysis and discussions with trusted friends, I did begin to consider leaving the country. I realized that my family would undergo trauma. Walter (thirteen) and Edward (eleven), our sons, had never been told of my Jewish origin. My wife and I wanted to spare them the trouble of the anti-Semitism so prevalent in Poland. The boys learned from their school-mates and neighbors that to be a Jew was something bad. Going to Israel, the only official avenue for emigration, would have meant revealing to them the situation we were in, and that could have been a severe shock.

I was not sure what my wife's reaction would be to a suggestion that we leave Poland. I suspected that she would be against emigration. After all, Zina had grown up in a system in which going to a capitalist country was consid-ered dreadfully wrong. Moreover, going to Israel, a country the Soviet Union labeled an "aggressor" and had severed diplomatic relations with, would seem almost treasonable. Besides, emigration could mean (and it actually did, until the demise of the Soviet Union) that she would not be allowed to visit her mother, sister, and other relatives in the USSR. Yet to my pleased surprise, Zina immediately agreed to emigration. She well understood what was going on in Poland and that the only sensible response was to leave. There was an additional reason. During her life in Poland, Zina had often encountered hos-tility directed at Soviet citizens and Russians in particular. Sadly, Poland and Russia had been enemies for centuries, and hostility remained high.

To apply for emigration also meant losing our jobs. And if our application was rejected, it could put us in a very precarious position. Hardship could also result from a delay in permission to emigrate. Even if we successfully over-came these hurdles, a big question remained as to how the Soviet embassy would react to Zina's application, since she was a Soviet citizen.

The emigration office was located in the Palac Mostowskich, a place noto-rious as the site of interrogations by the secret police. Nobody liked to go there. After receiving the permission, I would have to go to the Dutch em-bassy, which represented Israel's interests after Poland had severed diplomatic relations with it. If going to the Palac Mostowskich was unpleasant, going to a capitalist country's embassy was scary because of the way the police state regarded people who dealt with unfriendly foreign countries. But this was still ahead of me. Before I could take these steps I had to overcome an unexpected problem.

We quit our jobs at the Planning Commission, Zina went with the children to Moscow for a month for a last visit with her mother, and I was preparing the documents for the Palac Mostowskich. I then learned that the application required a photograph of me with the children. How could I produce such a photo when they were away? Delaying the whole procedure for a month was out of the question. I decided a photo montage from individual pictures would have to be tried. Then I had to find a photo laboratory I could trust not to denounce me for forgery. I was afraid to submit a false document. However, the officer at the Palac Mostowskich didn't pay any attention to the doctored photo. All they really cared about was that we were going to leave and our jobs and apartment might become available for their relatives or cronies.

Zina returned to Poland on August 21, that infamous day when the Soviet army, together with Poland and other Warsaw Pact countries, invaded Czechoslovakia. The next task facing us was to apply at the Soviet embassy for Zina's permission to emigrate to Israel. This was the scariest part. We tried to anticipate their reaction; we were prepared for a harsh reprimand and weren't sure she would actually get the permission. We decided on a low-key approach, in which Zina would agree with their political admonitions, but would claim that it was her husband and the father of her children who decided to emigrate and that she had to follow. I went with her to the Soviet embassy to provide support if needed.

Zina calmly said that she was applying to emigrate to Israel, and the secretary at the entry desk asked for her Soviet identity papers. With that document the secretary went into an adjoining room. Within a few seconds she returned, handed Zina her document and turned to the next person. We asked her what to do next, and the secretary answered: "That's it. You have permission to go." We were completely surprised. This was probably the fastest response the Soviet (or any other) bureaucracy had ever made. Hallelujah! We were on our way to freedom.

Many years later, I read an account of the events of 1968 in Poland that speculated that the anti-Semitic policy was orchestrated by the Soviets. I don't believe that. However, the behavior of the Soviet embassy in Warsaw clearly indicated that, not only were they not surprised by Zina's desire to leave, but that they were likely waiting for her. The procedure was worked out in advance and was made as easy as possible. That could only happen if they wanted us to emigrate. In this sense, and maybe in many others, the Soviets were a party to events in Poland.

Within a short time we received travel documents from the Polish authorities, stating that I was stateless as I had to renounce Polish citizenship as a condition of getting permission to emigrate. We were allowed to go only to

Israel because the authorities could thereby maintain the policy of preventing non-Jewish citizens from leaving. That was also the way the authorities implemented Gomulka's belief that Jews should have only one Fatherland, either Poland or Israel. The few other Polish citizens permitted to emigrate did not have to renounce citizenship. It meant more hardship for us since we would be stateless, and therefore defenseless until we obtained sponsorship. The authorities allowed us to exchange the equivalent of five dollars per person for travel.

We started to prepare for departure, limiting our luggage to absolute necessities, selling everything we had or giving it away. But we couldn't part with the books accumulated over the years. Each book we wanted to take with us had to be listed and presented to the customs agency for approval. While we were working on that list, our older son Walter glanced at it one day and realized that we were going to Israel. He remained calm and didn't show any signs of disapproval. Edward was told we were going on a trip around the world and was excited about it. Disappointment came later. In general, my wife and I kept our plans private in order to avoid unnecessary comments from unfriendly people.

We had to present to the customs authorities all our family photos, both prints and negatives. A few photos were seized; one was a picture of the Hungarian Parliament building in Budapest, in front of which a military band played to welcome a foreign ambassador as a group of kindergarten children passed nearby. The photo qualified as a picture of a military object. No wonder! Some twelve years earlier in 1956, Soviet tanks were battling Hungarian freedom fighters in that very place. We were also prevented from taking a copy of the party publication of Gomulka's speech at the 1956 October Central Committee meeting in which he criticized Poland's subordination to the Soviet Union.

The custom officers were unpleasant, rude, nasty, and corrupt. They extorted money or valuables before they would allow departing emigrants to take their possessions with them. And even that didn't guarantee that the next custom control station wouldn't require a new bribe. We didn't have much trouble with them because we didn't have much with us. From cashing in our savings and the money we realized from the sale of our furniture and belongings, we bought a set of silverware that we could legally take out of the country. We intend to pass it on, from generation to generation, as a family memento.

My brother Sam and his family were spared the agonies of 1968. They were harassed economically throughout the 1950s. Sam was living and working in the one-room apartment on Kamienna #3, where I met Bronia in 1946. He raised a family there. Their daughter Mary was born in 1947 and Simon in 1953. Sam manufactured hats, but the authorities tried to eradicate any private enterprise and their favored method was to increase taxes capriciously. Realizing that there was no future in Poland for him and his family, Sam immigrated to Australia in 1961 thus avoiding the 1968 turmoil.

4
Freedom at Last

26
Vienna and Rome
Refugees Again

Our train departed from the Warsaw-Gdansk station. For some time it had been a place where heart-breaking scenes of departing parents or children took place. Each day, many of the dwindling Jewish community assembled there to say goodbye to relatives and friends and, invariably, the departing people intoned the Israeli anthem when the train to Vienna left the station.

We had been there a few times to see friends off, but on October 28, 1968, it was our turn to wave from inside the train to well-wishers on the platform. It was not an ordinary farewell, in which people expect to meet again. We were parting from a country that was our home, where the ashes of our parents and relatives were spread, the country I had fought for and helped rebuild. It is not easy to leave a birthplace; yet we felt that a great injustice had been done to us and, before us, to our parents and relatives. We were leaving without knowing where this wandering would lead us. We left many friends with whom we had shared our lives for many years and whom we had relied on in difficult times. There were tears in their eyes and in ours.

The final whistle was sounded, and our journey into the unknown began. We were still not entirely free. The last customs control point on the Poland-Czechoslovakia border still awaited us and, after that, a last stretch through Czechoslovakia. Our gloom caused by the farewell was mixed with both fear of the difficulties of the immediate day and with hope for a better future in the free world. After a two-hour layover at the border with Czechoslovakia, we finally entered that country. By evening, we approached the border with Austria, and our excitement increased. Here came our freedom! We opened a bottle of champagne when the train reached the bridge over the Danube. Similar celebrations were taking place in other cars of the train. We felt like we had thrown off the yoke of many years of persecution and deprivation of basic human rights. Now we were free, even though we didn't know how we would manage life the very next day. We were happy, and that's what counted. The next day we arrived in Vienna in the early morning. Before leaving the train, Austrian officials came in to collect our travel documents. Jewish activists from *Sochnut*, an Israeli organization, welcomed us and took care of our immediate needs. There were also representatives from HIAS, the Hebrew Immigrant Aid Society. We started refugee life in a small hotel in downtown Vienna.

At first I felt diminished by having to depend on a relief organization. In a large room, hundreds of refugees tried to reach relief officials who distributed small amounts of money to allow a hand-to-mouth existence. It was not so much the small sums that depressed me, as much as the situation that I suddenly realized we were in. We gained freedom in exchange for misery.

After a few days in Vienna, we went to the *Sochnut* office to reclaim the travel documents taken from us by the police. We were supposed to go to Israel, as the destination in those documents stated. I had prepared an explanation for declining this opportunity, arguing that my wife was not Jewish, that she wouldn't feel comfortable there. I then realized how offensive this argument might sound to an Israeli. The *Sochnut* official pointed out that there were many such families in Israel, and that they were very happy. He said, "Bring her in; we'll talk to her, and I am sure that we can dispel any doubts she might have." Then I advanced another argument. I said, "I don't feel comfortable in a country with a hot climate." He replied, "But we have places where it is not so hot. For example, Jerusalem has a very mild climate." We argued a little bit more for a while, and the *Sochnut* representative finally gave in. "Here are your documents, but if you change your mind, Israel will be glad to receive you." I have to admit that, deep in my heart, I agreed with him, and it was an uncomfortable conversation. I admired Israel and was proud of its achievements, but I saw our place being somewhere else, although I didn't yet know where. The situation reminded me of a Jewish joke: A Jew went to a travel agency looking for a place to emigrate. They showed him many countries on a globe: Israel, France, Madagascar, China, and so on. None of them suited him. Finally he asked: "Do you have another globe?"

After a fortnight in Vienna, we were sent on to Rome, where HIAS had its headquarters. Here, operations were much better organized and the treatment of the refugees gentler. The *pensione* where we were placed furnished us with food and shelter, but the manager let us know that he was doing us a favor. HIAS found this place, which didn't cost much, and the manager behaved accordingly. Most people left the *pensione* after a few weeks. The room we then rented on Principie Eugenio turned out to be even worse. It was a nice space in a newly renovated apartment, but we were allowed one short shower per week and could cook only thirty minutes per day. After one week the owner told us that we would have to leave by the end of the month.

I started looking for another place to rent. Every day, from morning until evening, I walked the streets of Rome, searching for signs announcing the availability of a rental unit. The trouble was that, in most cases, I couldn't understand what they were telling me. Moreover, most of places required an annual lease, but we couldn't sign a contract for such a long time, since we hoped to get a departure visa in a few months. I walked the streets of Rome for almost three weeks without result. The situation became desperate. When I came home at the end of the day, Zina would be crying. In the end, I had to agree to rent a room in another *pensione*. There, at least, we were allowed to cook. With a place to live we could concentrate on improving our English and building plans for a new life.

The HIAS still took care of our immediate needs. The gentleman who dispensed aid was pleasant. Although it was difficult to reach him, when one did get his attention, he was a treasure. He understood each family's situation, and while staying within the limits of his authority he had a charming manner that didn't make his charges feel like beggars. That was not always the case with aid officials. We received an allowance of the equivalent of one hundred dollars per person per month to pay for all our expenses: food, shelter, and everything else. We got an additional amount for transportation to school, which we used to supplement other expenses, so we walked to school.

In response to a letter I sent to Anthony Hubert, secretary general of the EAPC (European Association of Productivity Centers), and a recommendation from friends in Czechoslovakia, Hubert suggested I write two papers for EAPC on productivity problems, for which I would be paid several hundred dollars. I was very happy, since, in addition to the much-needed money, it also gave me an opportunity to regain my professional self-esteem and to become better known among Western experts in my field. Hubert also arranged with the Italian Productivity Center to allow me to use their office. The director of the center received me warmly. This was most fortunate, as the center was just three hundred yards from the *pensione* where we lived.

Adam Jozefowicz, my friend and colleague from the Polish Planning Commission, was in Pakistan while we were in Rome. He kindly sent me a few hundred dollars and promised that his sister in London would get in touch with us. She did, and she was of great assistance. Her friends, the Szczepaniaks, lived in Rome and invited us to their house, showing great warmth and understanding of our plight. We visited them whenever they could find time. Mr. Szczepaniak, an economist, gave us good advice and many contacts in the United States. One of those was Professor Fritz Machlup, a world-renowned economist at Princeton University. Szczepaniak also introduced me to Mr. Wyczalkowski, a Polish economist who worked at the World Bank in Washington, D.C., together with our good friend from Lodz, Heniek Francuz.

The HIAS was very efficient in preparing our documents for the U.S. authorities in Rome. The main problem was that many of us, including myself, had at some time belonged to the Polish Workers Party, the Communist organization. U.S. law prohibited Communists from entering the country unless they could prove that they had joined the party involuntarily or that they had left it more than ten years earlier. The HIAS was preparing papers, which provided evidence that the applicant met these exceptions. In some cases, when it was impossible to do so, they advised the individual to apply to immigrate to Canada, Australia, or Sweden—countries without such prohibition.

It took at least two months after the submission of the application to be called for an interview with the U.S. consul. Another important hurdle was the medical examination. With tuberculosis, glaucoma, or venereal disease, chances were slim of being allowed to immigrate to the United States. An x-ray found some calcification on my lungs, which looked suspicious. I never had tuberculosis, and the Italian doctor diagnosed it as a benign condition. However, we didn't know how the U.S. authorities would interpret the x-ray. We were very concerned, since rejection could mean more suffering for the entire family.

Mrs. Szczepaniak introduced us to her friends, a Jewish woman from Poland and her Italian son-in-law. Theirs was an affluent family, and they treated us like their own. For the first time in our lives, we were invited to a Christmas celebration, with a beautifully decorated tree under which gifts from Santa awaited each member of our family. We used to have decorated trees at New Year's instead of Christmas, but never had gifts under the tree.

Mrs. Szczepaniak had another Christmas surprise for us. She organized a meeting for the Jewish refugees with a bishop of Rome. The bishop was very warm to us. He wished us all the best and showed a deep sympathy for our plight. This was the first and only time we had such a friendly, warm reception from a Catholic bishop.

Traditionally, we celebrated the coming of the New Year, and we intended to make no exception for this one in Rome. In Poland, we used to go to some large party or assemble in a private place with friends and dance until sunrise. With our meager resources in Rome we got together with a few friends, the Temkins, the Zachariaszes, the Eisenbergs; although it was a subdued celebration, we remember it for its unusual circumstances. Local people told us to be very careful walking the streets that night because we could be killed. "By whom?" we asked. "Aren't the Italians all in a good mood? Why do they want to kill somebody?" "No, you don't understand. There is a custom here on New Year's Eve; people throw all kinds of old furniture and appliances out their windows. You might be killed by such a flying object." We didn't truly believe it, but just in case we walked only in the middle of the street. When we returned home the next morning, we saw how true the warning was. The streets were littered with broken glass, furniture, dishwashers, and refrigerators. What a custom!

It reminded me of one New Year's party at Warsaw Polytechnic. The place was beautiful. There were thousands of people, not all students, and the music was too loud for our ears. At midnight, bottles and glasses started flying from the balconies of the round hall, down on the floor where we were supposed to dance. We had never seen such behavior at a New Year's ball. After half an hour of such destruction, the organizers apologized for the ordeal. It turned out that a large group of East German students were the glass throwers. We left immediately.

Many of the refugee children loved Rome. They had a good time walking the streets, window shopping, sometimes even buying an inexpensive toy. Adults often went with the children to the markets, enjoying the rich variety of fruits and vegetables and the frequent invitations to buy them. The oranges were *la bellas* (the beauties), and one could buy a whole kilogram for a hundred lira. My job was to buy groceries. The store across the street had huge pieces of Parmesan and other cheeses displayed at the store entrance. Inside, the selection of cheeses and other delicacies was enormous; we weren't used to so many choices. The salesman met me with a smile, and, after observing me for a long time, during which I was trying to figure out the names and prices, he finally asked, "Do you speak English?" "Yes," I answered, happy that

I would be able to have some help. Then he responded, "I don't." Although I was disappointed, I laughed.

In the beginning of 1969 we were called for an interview at the U.S. consulate. It was a pleasant interview, where I stated all the reasons for being a member of the party and what I did in Poland. The consul liked my explanation that I had been a sort of dissident, a revisionist trying to change the dictatorial system. I told him that it was my own decision to turn in my membership card—in other words, that I quit that gang on my own. Zina had an even easier time with the consul, since she never had been a party member and had left the *Komsomol* youth organization many years before. We awaited the decision.

We got a positive response from the U.S. consul. A charter flight was scheduled for the end of February. On the indicated date, we assembled at a plaza in downtown Rome. There were a lot of people loading their luggage atop a bus that would take us to the airport. Many of our friends came to help and to say goodbye. This time it was not a sad farewell. Some rather envied us as we were going, while they would have to wait in uncertainty. There was a lot of commotion and a little bit of chaos. But somehow we got loaded on the bus and started our journey to the land of opportunity. Our spirits were high and we hoped for a better future. Friends wished us good luck. They shouted, "Earn a thousand dollars a month." It was a modest sum, but to us it sounded like a million.

Boarding the plane at the airport was even more chaotic than loading the bus. We were flying with a large group of peasants from Yugoslavia. They knew nothing about civilized behavior and were pushing aboard as if their lives depended on it. We decided to wait until things settled down, so we boarded the plane last, a little nervous whether we would get a seat. When we entered the plane, all the coach-class seats were already occupied. The crew decided to give us first-class seats. Hurray, we were going to the United States in style!

27
New York and Princeton
Vistas of Opportunity

We arrived in New York late in the afternoon of February 14, 1969, at JFK Airport, and we were met by our cousin Fred Heller, his wife Dina, and their two children, Peter and David. After getting our luggage, they drove us to the Coliseum Hotel, on Seventy-first Street in Manhattan. Thus began our new life in the United States. Our cousins were very gracious and helpful. We got some financial support from the New York Association for New Americans (NYANA), a Jewish institution devoted to assisting refugees from Communist countries. Needless to say, our situation was precarious. We didn't know the customs of the country or how and where to look for employment, and we definitely didn't like to depend on handouts from relief institutions. Hence, we immediately started looking for jobs with the help of our cousin Fred.

We learned very soon that the search for a professional job involves many meetings and interviews, during which the number of people contacted grows exponentially. Some of those meetings ended with a lunch, which was very nice but it usually meant no job offer. Letters sent out to prospective employers elicited pleasant responses such as, "Currently, there is no opening, but we're impressed with your qualifications and will keep your resume in our active files."

A meeting with Dr. Greenberg, an official with the U.S. Labor Department, was very productive. I had met Dr. Greenberg at a United Nations conference of productivity experts in Geneva in 1961. He remembered me and provided a list of people to contact in New York. The International Ladies Garment Workers Union was on his list; I went there for an interview, at which I was questioned about my knowledge of price indices. It was a very easy test, and I was offered a job with a weekly salary of $165.

Simultaneously, I approached an organization that assisted refugees with professional training. There I had several interviews, each time with another caseworker or a supervisor. I became desperate, because time was passing and my prospects looked bleak. I argued that I had experience in various industries, including coal mining, textiles, and construction. One call to G. A. Hanscomb Partnership, an international company, led to a meeting with its manager, Raymond Firmin. After some discussions, I was offered a job as an economist at $200 a week. I accepted the offer happily.

A few weeks earlier, I had met Professor Fritz Machlup of Princeton University. He reviewed my credentials, liked my proficiency in English, and promised to write letters to several universities recommending me for a teaching position. As he escorted me to the door, Machlup said, "Goodbye, Dr. Broner." That was gracious of him, as in my resume, I indicated that I was only about to start doctoral studies at Warsaw University. I told him that I didn't have a Ph.D., but had been offered the opportunity to start graduate studies at the University of Kentucky. He responded, "Why not at Princeton?" My intuition prompted me to say yes—that I would be glad to attend, if possible. Dr. Machlup promised to talk to the director of the graduate program of the economics department, Dr. William Baumol, and he felt sure that the director would agree and that I would get application forms in a few days.

I was admitted to the graduate school at Princeton University. Professor Baumol invited us to Princeton to get acquainted. It was springtime, and Princeton was in full bloom. The minute my wife and I got off the bus and looked around, we fell in love with that small, serene, and beautiful university town.

I went back to Hanscomb to tell Ray Firmin that I had been admitted to Princeton University and wouldn't be able to accept the job he offered me. He could not believe what he heard. He was very happy for me. He told me that Princeton was a very prestigious university and that it was extremely difficult to get accepted there. He advised me to accept the offer, which I had already done. Ray suggested that I work in his office until September when the fall semester started at Princeton.

I started my new career as an economist at Hanscomb. For more than four months, I commuted from Princeton to New York, walking from the Port Authority terminal to the offices on Forty-second Street. Although it was very hot in the summer, I enjoyed those walks by the famous skyscrapers, watching the rushing, dynamic New Yorkers and the beautiful young girls.

My graduate studies at Princeton began in the fall of 1969. I didn't realize what it really meant to do graduate work at Princeton without having done undergraduate studies at a Western university. Quickly I understood that my studies of Marxist economics in Moscow were not helpful at all. As a matter of fact, Dr. Machlup stressed that the first thing I had to do was to forget everything I had learned there. Insufficient undergraduate preparation in free-market economics, almost complete lack of exposure to the mathematical basis of American economic literature, and my age (I was forty-four when I began at Princeton) were all major handicaps.

Despite all obstacles, I passed the general exams in the standard two years and got my master's degree. Then I continued work toward the Ph.D. I completed a dissertation on economic integration in Eastern Europe and was awarded a Ph.D. in Economics in 1975. I was probably the oldest graduate student at Princeton. It was a period of four years of extremely hard work that resulted in many doors opening for me in institutions of higher learning. However, instead of accepting a teaching position, I decided to join the New Jersey Office of Economic Policy. After a short period, at the recommendation of the state's Economic Policy Council, Governor Brendan T. Byrne named me director of that office and at the same time I became the executive secretary of the council. Both the council and office advised the governor and the legislature on the state's economic policy. Such institutions existed only in a few U.S. states, and in New Jersey it was considered to have a useful role.

In 1990, I retired from state government, moved to Florida, and started the next phase of my life, pursuing a new hobby of painting and writing this memoir.

28

The Rats Abandon the Sinking Ship

The Collapse of the Soviet Union

In the summer of 1991 Zina and I traveled to Moscow in the Russian Republic, where my wife's mother Agrypina and her sister Zhenia as well as other relatives lived. My late wife Zina visited them for the last time in 1968, almost twenty-three years before and thereafter could not get a visa to Poland and the Soviet Union. Now we both had U.S. passports.

The trip to Moscow was eventful beyond imagination. During our stay we witnessed the attempted coup d'etat against the Gorbachev government, the collapse of the Soviet Union, and the nascent democratic revolution in Russia. Who in his right mind could have predicted such a profound chain of events, among the most significant of the twentieth century?

Very early in the morning of August 19, 1991, I was awakened by a radio announcement that the president of the Soviet Union, Mikhail Gorbachev, was ill and that Vice President Gennadi Yanaev was taking over the president's functions. That wouldn't have been unusual or ominous. However, the next broadcast was a declaration of a state of emergency in the Soviet Union. From now on, the entire country was to be ruled by a Government Committee of State Emergency (GCSE) whose members were the deputy chairman of the USSR Defense Council, Baklanov; the chairman of the KGB (secret police), Kriuchkov; Prime Minister Pavlov; Minister of Internal Affairs Pugo; Defense Minister Yazov; Vice President Yanaev, and a few others.

It seemed very strange to me. Why did these people need another ruling arrangement, when all of them were already in power, in the highest and most important positions of government? Was it a coup to remove President Gorbachev?

I learned more of their real intentions from the following broadcasts and decrees: first, Lukyanov, chairman of the Supreme Soviet (not formally a member of the GCSE), issued a statement, dated August 16, criticizing the agreement of the Union of Sovereign States, reached among Mikhail Gorbachev, Boris Yeltsin, and representatives of the other Soviet Republics on how they would relate to one another in a reformed Soviet Union. That agreement was supposed to be signed on August 20, and the GCSE intended to prevent its signing. The junta wanted much less independence among the Republics, and a system closer to the old Soviet Union model of central planning and subordination.

In its appeal to the Soviet nation, the GCSE expressed unhappiness with the economic and political reforms of Gorbachev. They emphasized what they called mortal danger for the nation, claiming that extremists were bent on seizing power at any cost, leading to what they claimed would be liquidation of the Soviet Union and consequent chaos, insubordination, and apathy. In short, they tried to justify a return to a dictatorial, Stalinist government model. They phrased their argument in the terms of democracy and openness, glasnost and perestroika, thereby admitting that reform policies had appeal among the population.

The Soviet Union never had a violent coup d'etat. That form of governmental change was frequent in smaller, unstable nations, but never in the USSR. In the Soviet Union the military was always subordinate to the Communist Party. The members of the GCSE could have followed the usual practice in Communist countries of removing the general secretary of the party from his party and from government posts, and that would have been enough. One of the junta members could then have been "elected" as the new party general secretary, and the new group would have all the necessary authority to rule the country. As the junta decided to undertake a coup and declare a state of emergency, they were seeking more than just the removal of Gorbachev from power. The main obstacle to a return to a Stalinist government was Boris Yeltsin, the elected president of the Russian Republic. He was an anticommunist, determined to lead Russia toward a democratic market economy and away from the central command economy of the entire Soviet Union. The plotters had to get rid of Yeltsin. The situation was much different now than under the former regime; it would not be easy to return to a Stalinist system in a country already on the path to reform and democratic development. Only a coup d'etat could accomplish this. A Stalinist regime in power could have overcome any obstacles by a little terror.

The first order given by the KGB was to arrest Yeltsin. President Gorbachev was only declared "ill" and isolated in his vacation house in the Crimea. Some believe that Gorbachev's role in the coup remains a mystery. Coup participants Anatoly Lukyanov and Gennady Yanaev later claimed that Gorbachev knew of their plans from the very beginning. Lukyanov reported that Gorbachev simply wanted to assess the strength of the domestic opposition before returning to Moscow.

I was saddened to hear these ominous decrees. Despite the inconsistency of Gorbachev's reforms, they created the means whereby the Soviet people could gradually join the Western nations in freedom and economic growth. I shared my views with Zhenia, my wife's sister, and predicted that ten years of a painful Stalinist dictatorship faced the Soviet people. Zhenia disagreed. She believed the coup attempt would fail within a few days. I based my opinion on history, while Zhenia knew what the people in the street were thinking.

I took to the streets. On the main thoroughfare, heavy tanks moved. It was foreboding and scary. Muscovites were used to seeing tanks only for celebrations of May Day and the October Revolution, so why were they moving into the city now? Will there be shooting? At whom would they shoot? Could there be a civil war?

Defense Minister Yazov ordered Colonel General N. V. Kalinin, commander of the Moscow Military District, to bring the Taman motorized rifle division and the Kantemir tank division into Moscow to take up defensive positions at key intersections and institutions. This force amounted to some 4,600 combat troops, more than 300 tanks, some 420 armored vehicles, and 430 specially equipped cars.

I was afraid to take photographs of the tanks; I well remembered that up to Stalin's death nobody was allowed to take pictures of the Kremlin. Whenever someone took pictures a militiaman would ask for the camera. He would expose the negative, then return the camera with a warning not to take any more pictures. If the militia or undercover agents caught me, an American, taking pictures of tanks during a state of emergency, I could have been in big trouble. But they could not prevent me from registering in my memory the faces and reactions of ordinary Muscovites watching the tanks roll into the peaceful city. People were bewildered, watching quietly, their faces expressing grief and apprehension. I noticed neither approval nor resistance. Yet resistance was apparent and building up in other places near the Russian Parliament, known as the Russian White House.

The GCSE forbade publication of all independent newspapers. Only a few Communist-controlled papers appeared the next day with reports of the changes in the country. There were long lines in front of newsstands where only one paper, the *Workers Tribune,* was available. On the front page all the GCSE pronouncements and directives appeared. A short item on what was going on in Moscow during the first day of the state of emergency described a scene opposite the Hotel Moskva, in the very center of the city. It read: "On the top of two trolley buses, young people waved the white, blue and red flag of Russia." A caption stated that Yeltsin had called for a general strike and a rally at the huge Manezh Plaza. That was shocking. Why did a junta-controlled paper print a story of coup opponents calling for resistance under the banner of the Russian flag? The only explanation I could think of was that the junta was not entirely in control. Later in the day I saw resistance building, but it was not prevented by the authorities. Who were the authorities anyway? Clearly, the junta had not gotten the upper hand in the streets of Moscow.

Similar appeals for disobedience to the junta were issued by President Yeltsin and were posted at many Moscow Metro stations throughout the city. With the arrival of each subway train, people leaving the station stopped to read the appeals posted on the walls. There were Yeltsin's proclamations and other clandestinely printed statements. Where were the militia to prevent or remove such unauthorized material from the Metro's walls? What surprised me most was that nobody interfered with people reading those proclamations. Was this how the state of emergency was being implemented and enforced? Was this how the mighty Soviet government enforced its commands? It was clear the junta could not enforce its orders. I surmised that the junta was cautious; they probably did not want to frighten people yet. They wanted to arrest Yeltsin and then be free to deal with the population.

My prediction was that the day after the coup there would be plenty of food in Moscow stores. That was the way the Soviet government sought to gain favor with the population. In this case, they clearly needed it. Zhenia again corrected me. "You will see no more food, and shortages everywhere." Zhenia was right again. The junta's statement was that within two weeks an inventory of supplies would be available for the GCSE. But the prime minister of the USSR was on the junta; didn't he already know the supply situation? The world press predicted shortages and even famine in parts of the Soviet Union. Was it possible that coup leaders really didn't have enough control to affect the supply of food, even in Moscow alone?

Even before arriving in Moscow, I had a clear sense of the weakened power of the Communist Party, and I presumed that the only viable remaining force in the Soviet Union was the military. Zhenia again corrected me. "No," she answered, "you have out-of-date ideas. Our army is not the same as it was. Officers are not getting paid; their families are without the money to buy basic provisions. They are disappointed and discouraged, especially those that participated in the war in Afghanistan." The next day or two would reveal the army's role in that critical moment.

Secret KGB units were given orders to arrest President Yeltsin and to take over the Russian Parliament building. From an interview with KGB commander Karpuchin on August 24, the correspondent of the *Literaturnaya Gazieta* learned that he and his men decided not to follow the orders, considering them illegal. They surrounded the villa where President Yeltsin stayed, but let him leave the compound on the way to the Russian White House. General Karpuchin's unit had a strength of 15,000, and the decision to disobey the order was courageous and risky. For the leaders of the coup, this disobedience created a serious problem. Nevertheless, they tried to use other motorized divisions to storm the White House the next evening.

In the meantime, thousands of Muscovites and soldiers who had served in the war in Afghanistan organized the defense of the White House and its approaches. Construction workers hauled in heavy concrete slabs and put them on roads leading to the White House: a ring of barricades surrounded the approaches to the White House, where the leadership of Russia concentrated. Some military units switched allegiance to Yeltsin. The president himself jumped on top of a tank in front of the White House on the first day of the coup and called on the people not to obey orders of the junta and to join a general strike.

The critical moment came on the night of August 21. Tank units took up positions not far from the White House with orders to storm the parliament building during the night. On one of the main streets of Moscow a tragedy occurred. Civilians tried to stop the advancing armored units. The latter started shooting and three young men, Dimitri Komar, Ilya Krychevsky, and Vladimir Usov, were killed. Even though Krychevsky was Jewish, his parents decided that he should be buried with his fellows as a symbol of national unity. The next morning, massive indignation against the junta and support for Yeltsin was evident. Proclamations from the Russian president and the underground newspapers were everywhere. In front of a building where an ad hoc independent newspaper was being published, hundreds gathered to read the latest news. On the streets I could see the intense expressions on the faces of Muscovites, worrying about their future and at the same time openly disobedient to the GCSE. Widespread expressions of mourning for the victims of the junta was seen in thousands of bouquets spread along the street where the tragedy occurred. Banners on top of the flowers read: "True sons of Russia, who fell in the struggle against the communist dictatorship." It became clear that the coup had inaugurated a struggle of democratic forces against the Communist regime.

Shivers ran up my spine when I saw groups of young people carrying Russian flags toward the Moscow Soviet building. I was afraid for them. It was a surreal picture, and I felt that I was witnessing a new Russian Revolution. The junta could have considered it a counterrevolution, and the reaction could have been deadly. But those young men were running forward, paying no attention to anybody. The next day, when I returned, the Russian white-blue-red flag flamed on top of the Moscow Soviet building.

In the afternoon of August 21 Zhenia got a call from a friend who reported: "The rats are abandoning the sinking ship." Some of the junta's leaders, including Lukyanov, the Supreme Soviet's chairman, were flying out of Moscow. It looked like the coup was dead; its leaders were on the run. We learned what had happened a few hours later. Some junta leaders decided to go to Foros in the Crimea, where President Gorbachev was under house arrest. It was not clear whether they wanted Gorbachev to join them or at least to justify their actions, thereby saving them from severe punishment if they failed. Gorbachev would not see them. Then members of President Yeltsin's government, including his vice president, Rutskoy, flew to Foros to bring Gorbachev back to Moscow. He returned on the morning of August 22.

That day all the independent newspapers were again published. I went early in the morning to the nearest newsstand and bought copies of almost all the papers, even those still controlled by the Communists. I was astonished by how suddenly the party-controlled publications reversed course, now condemning the coup and criticizing such means of solving the country's problems. Zina and I went into town and this time I recorded in my camera the mountains of flowers spread where the three young men were killed. Zina was moved and shaken by those scenes. She was saddened by what was happening. This was her country and Moscow the city where she lived until we married and left for Poland. As a teenager, she worked here during the war, producing automatic rifles and contributing to the survival of her homeland. And now it seemed to her that the country was falling apart. Maybe from a different angle, I also worried about Russia. I always had good feelings toward the Russian people. This was the country that saved my life. It had also put a rifle in my hand, which I used to fight the Germans. Maybe I even received one of the weapons that Zina helped produce. My mother-in-law, Agrypina, worried mainly about the danger of fraternal fighting. She viewed Gorbachev's reforms as too fast and incomprehensible.

The revolutionary fervor strengthened, spread throughout the city, and emboldened the population. The main targets were now the monuments of Bolshevik leaders. I went to the statue of Felix Dzerzhinsky, the Polish communist who headed the secret police in the first years of the Communist regime. His monument was in front of the KGB building where the infamous Lubyanka prison was also located. When I arrived at the plaza, the tall figure of Dzerzhinsky had already been torn from its large base. I learned that initially Muscovites themselves tried to knock it down. Moscow city officials urged people not to pull down the heavy bronze figure that could endanger bystanders and damage the street and the subway right beneath it. They promised to bring appropriate equipment and remove it safely, which they did. When I went to the front door of the KGB building, I noticed a polite sign saying: "The Committee of State Security (KGB). Open to citizens 24 hours a day." How subtle! Probably the only institution that worked so hard!

I also visited a place not far from the Hotel Moskva, where a small monument to Yakov Svierdlov, first president (actually the chairman of the Supreme Soviet), had stood. It was also gone. I felt some sentiment, not for Yakov Svierdlov, but for his brother, whose name I had forgotten. When I was a student in Moscow in the early 1950s, Yakov's brother used to visit our dormitory, *Dom Communy*, and give an account of the international situation. He was a high functionary of the Ministry of Foreign Affairs, and there was always a standing-room-only crowd of students because he was such a good lecturer, often providing information not published in the papers. Although he did not deviate far from the party line, his presentations were stylish and delivered in vivid, beautiful Russian. We enjoyed them very much.

The anticommunist revolution was spreading. At about the same time that Dzerzhinsky's statue was removed from the front of the KGB building, we learned that Marshal Shaposhnikov, who had joined the Yeltsin forces very early, was appointed defense minister of the USSR. On August 23, at a staff meeting of the air force, he ordered the depoliticization of the military and renounced his membership in the Communist Party. The assembled officers warmly applauded his action. Similarly, Communists from the central KGB office voted to leave the party. Did I believe them? Maybe not, but it showed the panic that engulfed even the most untouchable servants of old Soviet regime. Yeltsin, in the presence of Gorbachev, signed a decree ordering the cessation of activities of the Russian Communist Party. The newspaper *Pravda* ceased to be published. Two prominent coup leaders, Marshal Akhromeev and Interior Minister Pugo, committed suicide.

In a few days news reached Moscow that major union republics, among them Ukraine, Belorussia, Kazakhstan, and the Baltic republics of Lithuania, Latvia, and Estonia, had declared their independence. Although many issues remained to be resolved, among them economic integration and military organization, for all practical purposes the Soviet Union, as we knew it, ceased to exist.

I thought of a story I used to tell: "At a coffee shop in Paris, a Russian refugee came in one morning and ordered a cup of coffee and the newspaper *Pravda*. The waiter brought the coffee and said that *Pravda* was not published anymore and that the Soviet Union was dissolved. The next morning the same customer came in and ordered coffee and *Pravda*. The waiter brought the coffee and gave the same report about *Pravda* and the Soviet Union. After several more days of the same routine, the waiter got annoyed and told the customer, "Sir, you seem to be an intelligent person. Why do you always order the same thing, knowing that we don't have it?" "It's simple," the customer answered, "I'm so happy to hear the same answer over and over again."

Well, this was only a joke designed to wake up my audience, in case they were falling asleep, while I spoke of economic policy in the United States and in New Jersey. But in Moscow, all the elements of that joke actually took place, and I saw it myself. They were extraordinary events that removed the danger of nuclear conflagration and opened the road to freedom and prosperity for the Russian people. I was extremely happy to be there in those days that again shook the world and to see it all happen in front of my eyes.

29
Pilgrimage to the Past—Kamiensk, the Shtetl

We decided to visit Kamiensk—a small *shtetl* in Poland where my ancestors used to live. We approached the village of Kamiensk with great trepidation. About fifty-five years had passed since I had been there. A terrible war and social and ethnic upheaval had taken place since, and Kamiensk certainly wasn't left unscathed. It wasn't easy to imagine how the village would look. Would reality resemble the pictures stored away in my memory? Would I be disappointed? I didn't expect to find family there. But would I recognize the buildings where my grandparents and our family lived so many years ago? Would the oversized Kosciuszko monument, associated with so many happy days of my childhood, still be there? These and many other questions were running through my mind as we approached in a dilapidated Polish car nicknamed the *maluch* (midget). Most stressful was the impending confrontation with the place and people that probably witnessed the last days of my family. I hadn't been able to face that horrible truth for many years, while many of the witnesses were still alive. In 1991, after being away from Poland for more than twenty-three years, I finally made a pilgrimage to that graveyard.

Kamiensk holds a very important place in the long history of the Ginats, my mother's ancestors. I knew her parents lived there, and while searching my roots, I made many discoveries about my ancestors going back to the end of the eighteenth century. It surprised me to learn that my father's roots also led to Kamiensk; many generations of Broners lived there as well. Simon, my paternal grandfather, was born in Kamiensk, and his parents moved to Lodz in the mid-nineteenth century. Only recently did I discover that my maternal grandma Blima was also a Broner. There must have been many gravestones for Ginats and Broners in that little town.

Kamiensk was a typical quiet Polish town with a relatively large plaza in the center, surrounded by single-story houses. The center of the square was dominated by the monument to Tadeusz Kosciuszko, Poland's national hero, leader of the insurrection against Russian occupation at the end of the eighteenth century, and also renowned in the United States for his participation in the American Revolution. A large Roman Catholic Church stood across from the monument, and nearby was the house where my grandparents used to live.

On Wednesdays, the plaza served as a marketplace. Farmers from nearby villages brought their produce to town and artisans exhibited their goods. Somewhere in that crowd was my mother, selling hats my father made. Times were very hard. My parents had moved the family to Kamiensk, about sixty miles from Lodz, while Father remained in the city where he could get the cloth for the hats he made. I remembered his imitation astrakhan caps, about ten inches high, which were good in the severe winters. Mother would sell those hats, standing the whole day in the cold waiting for customers who came to buy late, after having earned money from sale of their produce.

In addition to that vivid picture of Mother, I remembered a few more scenes of our family life. I see a picture in my memory, when Father joined us for a religious holiday, of Mother complaining about the miserable life the family was leading. As much as I can reconstruct, before the 1929 Depression our family enjoyed a relatively prosperous life. The change for the worse was very hard on Mother.

Wednesday fairs were a source of excitement, provided by Leibl, the son of the town's *shoichet* (kosher butcher). He was a kleptomaniac, going out regularly to steal fruits and vegetables from the farmers' stalls. Often farmers would catch him and beat him up. His screaming was so loud and dramatic that from afar one would believe that this time he was really being drubbed. Within a couple of hours, the same screams would fill the little town again. He was back at it, undaunted.

I was sent to a *cheder* (school) to learn the Torah when I was less than five years old. The little school was near my grandparents' house, on the second floor of a dilapidated building. We learned to read of the Hebrew prayers and the Torah. The *melamed* (teacher) was poor, as were the parents of his pupils, who paid him little for his services, if he got that.

In the summer of 1930 when I was five years old, Mother gave birth to my youngest brother, her seventh and last child. Every afternoon after school, the whole class would run across the plaza to the street where our family lived, knock at the door, and even before the door was opened, start singing a blessing. All of us, including myself, were well rewarded. Partly in consequence, I loved my baby brother very much.

On his eighth day of life, a traditional *bris* ceremony was held in our home, attended by many guests, whereupon the baby was circumcised and named Yitzhak. I remember a barrel of beer and guests pumping it into glasses. There was plenty of food, and at the end of the celebration everybody waited for the waffle cake, made in the shape of a bowl. People broke off pieces of the waffle, laughing and talking and having a good time. I don't know whether the waffle had a special meaning, but at some point during the party it became the center of attention. Those were the pictures that popped up in my memory on the way to Kamiensk in the summer of 1991.

We hoped that our visit might shed some light on the fate of my parents and siblings during the German occupation. As expected, the place looked much smaller now than I remembered it. The plaza was small, the church remained, and the Kosciuszko monument was no longer there, but a group of workmen were at work building a new monument. When we asked what they were building, they jokingly said: "Maybe it will be a monument to Lech Walesa, president of the new Poland. No, actually we're restoring the original monument of Kosciuszko." Then we met the chairman of the restoration committee and the mayor of Kamiensk. After introductions, I asked whether any of them remembered my grandfather, the glazier who lived near the church. They were too young to remember people from the prewar years, but suggested we talk to Mr. Sowinski, who knew a lot about those years. We also learned that there existed a historical society, which published material about old Kamiensk (including a picture of the old Kosciuszko monument).

We moved on to Mr. Sowinski's house. He wasn't there; it was harvest time and people were in the field digging potatoes. His daughter, a charming young lady, promised to help us find people who might know something about our family. She also confirmed that her father was familiar with events during the war and promised to walk us to the potato field as soon as she completed her chores.

In the meantime, we returned to the marketplace to visit the house where my grandparents lived before the war. Luckily it was still there. In 1939, at the beginning of the German invasion, policemen from Kamiensk decided to oppose the German bombers flying over the village, firing their rifles at the Luftwaffe planes. Within a short time, some bombers flew over the village and destroyed several buildings adjacent to my grandparents' house. Since their house remained intact and we hadn't heard at the time about any casualties, we surmised that our grandfather survived that attack. (Later I learned from Sam that our grandma Blima died before the war, which I hadn't known.)

I went into the house where I thought my grandparents had lived. The place looked different. I remembered a narrow long room about three by ten yards. Grandpa would get up very early in the morning, put on his *tefilin* (phylacteries—little black boxes containing a scroll of the *Shema* prayer), and begin to pray. He walked in the room saying the prayers so fast that I could barely distinguish any particular word, at the same time shaking a bottle of sour cream to make fresh butter. Now there wasn't a living room, instead it was a small village store, whose owner told us that she acquired it in the 1960s and that she did not know anything about how the place looked before. She was very reserved in her answers and wanted to know who we are, what we were looking for, and whether we had owned the place before the war. We assured her that we did not and that we were only looking at it because my grandparents had lived there.

Later on, we moved to the other end of the plaza, where the intercity bus used to stop and where a gasoline pump was located. The pump was gone, but a group of elderly people was standing there. Yes, they recalled the gasoline pump, and that Jews in Kamiensk didn't own properties (we hadn't asked that question), but mostly rented. That may have been so, but why was everybody so concerned about who owned what? We realized after a few more conversations that property restitution has become a very sensitive issue after the abolition of the Communist regime. During the war, Poles had moved into the homes of deported Jews. Some atrocities were perpetuated by Poles immediately after the war when a few survivors claimed their lawful properties while the current occupiers refused to return them. After 1991 and especially with Poland's entry to the European Union, such claims by previous owners became more frequent and legally justified. However, Poland's government has not yet resolved this thorny issue.

Our next visit was to the manor where my sister Esther apparently worked in 1940. I hoped that we would find someone who had been there at the time. One worker, who had been employed in the manor all those years, was still there, but he remembered nothing. The only information we got was that an heir to the original Polish owner, who at the time of our visit lived in England,

had regained ownership of the manor, which was a state farm in the inter-
vening years. Apparently he had no difficulty in claiming his property.

The most fruitful visit was the one in the potato field. Mr. Sowinski was
very friendly, remembered much, and was willing to share the information
he had. He recalled knowing my grandpa, the glazier, but no particular events
related to him. He told us that the Germans had assembled the Jewish population of Kamiensk at the railroad ramp in Gorzkowice, a nearby village, for
transport to Treblinka. We also learned that other Jewish people originally
from Kamiensk had been to visit. After this meeting, we tried to find more
elderly people, but nobody was at home.

I confess the nostalgia overwhelmed me, and I couldn't resist entering the
house where my little school used to be held on the second floor. I found the
place, but it looked much smaller than I remembered it. The whole school,
consisting of about eight pupils, used to assemble around a low table in the
corridor, just after one climbed a set of ancient-looking stone stairs. I recalled
vividly the first exciting day in that school. The teacher held a little wooden
pointer, opened a book, and said, "This is the letter *alef* and the next is *beit*."
I think that every child in the world is excited at the first day in school, confronting that mysterious set of letters that will lead, eventually, to reading
beautiful stories in big books. Looking at my first school, I couldn't believe
that this was actually the same place, the one that so excited me more than
sixty years before.

We hoped that some official statistical documents might have been preserved, but were told that during the German occupation, the Polish underground destroyed all the Kamiensk documents to prevent the Nazis learning
the whereabouts of the men from particular households.

Then we moved to Gorzkowice. I easily found the place where my uncle
and aunt Pytkowski used to live. We came across a man who had lived there
all the time, and although he remembered the Pytkowskis, he didn't know
exactly what had happened to them. He corroborated the information we had
received from others: that the Jews were transported in boxcars to an unknown destination from the railway ramp in Gorzkowice. We went to that
place and tried to imagine the tragedy of our people, as they were loaded by
the German beasts, and sent away to the gas chambers in Treblinka.

Epilogue

Sixty years have passed since the end of WWII and the annihilation of six million Jews among other victims, including my family and a wide net of relatives. One might expect that after such a long period, grief would fade and that having my own family, children, and grandchildren would mute the pain of my loss. It would also seem that the postwar German government's recognition of that nation's guilt in murdering so many innocent people would incline one toward forgiveness. I cannot detect any such feelings in myself. The more time that goes by, the more resentment I feel, and I am not able to forgive. I am aware that many people would counsel that I be magnanimous, and look to the future instead of to the terrible past. They would argue that I should recognize that the majority of contemporary Germans had nothing to do with the atrocities perpetrated by their countrymen. In response to this reasoning I feel obliged to lay out my thinking, to open my inner thoughts to help explain if not justify my continuing grief and resentment.

The normal reaction to the death of a family member is shock and grief. Over time the healing process takes over, grief fades, and in most cases there is no reason to be angry toward anyone. But my pain and resentment increase over time. Initially I hoped that my loved ones would one day miraculously appear. That may explain why I did not go through a period of shock. I did not see, and still do not know, how they were murdered. Learning their likely fate filtered in slowly. The more I read eyewitness accounts of Nazi atrocities, about the slow process of dying under the dreadful conditions in the ghettos, the more I associated those accounts with what had been done to members of my own family. When I read that a Nazi or his collaborator had smashed a child's head on the cobblestones or shot someone at point-blank range, I think of my sister's child. When I read how the Nazis lured women to undress to take a shower in Treblinka, and instead of water turned on poison gas, I always think of my mother and sisters being there. I am unable to avoid these thoughts. The more I read such accounts, the more I hate the Nazis, and everyone who helped them in their heinous crimes. The death of my loved ones becomes more vivid, as if had just happened.

And it is not just anger. The more time I have to think about what happened, the more I learn from eyewitness accounts about the horrors of that insane regime, the less I am able to comprehend how so-called human beings could become such beasts and systematically kill millions of innocent people. I can't understand how the leaders of the free world could have been so indifferent when they learned what the Nazis were doing to the Jews. The governments of the free world, who were engaged in the struggle against the Nazis, knew early on what the Germans were doing in the extermination and concentration camps. They knew of the deprivation and starvation of the millions in the ghettos, who had no hope of survival. Emissaries from Poland and elsewhere reached Allied governments about the tragic conditions in the ghettos. Why didn't those governments speak out about Nazi atrocities? And as rumors and stories began to filter out of the ghettos and camps, how did those nations react to that grim news?

I don't intend to second-guess the motives of the free nations and their governments. I only want to understand. Think of it. In peacetime, whenever a tragedy happens to a single person or family, the media inform people, and they react sympathetically, rushing to provide assistance. I understand that a war was going on and that the free world was busy carrying on that war, bent on defeating the Nazis, and that goal governed all. But aid to the Jews and other victims should not have interfered with that goal. The unfortunate people in the extermination camps may have hoped the allies would bomb those camps, knowing that they might suffer as well. But they would have accepted that to see the destruction of the German machinery of death that consumed thousands every day.

I wonder how many banner headlines appeared in the leading newspapers of the free world about those atrocities. Apparently there were a few. And I am also willing to speculate that if such news stories were the order of the day, a different response from their governments and their armed forces would have followed.

Was the Jewish population living in the free allied nations sufficiently alarmed by the plight of their brethren under German occupation? It is known that efforts on behalf of the Jews were made by those in position to help. We also learn about noble non-Jews who risked their positions to send assistance to the endangered Jewish people. However, it remains that those efforts were far from sufficient.

My anger is appropriately directed to those bystanders and witnesses who could have done so much more to help their neighbors, especially in Poland. Again, there were hundreds, if not thousands, who risked their lives to help the Jews, hiding them, providing food, and even a few weapons to fight the Nazis. Unfortunately, they were a tiny minority. Most of the population in Poland was either indifferent or in many cases even assisted the occupiers in their campaign to exterminate the Jews. I am not able to understand why. Now that more and more eyewitness accounts are published on atrocities committed by Poles themselves, I am at a loss. What hate must have been planted and nourished in their minds to cause them to seize an opportunity to kill the Jewish neighbors with whom not long before they lived peacefully? At the end of 1968, at the height of the anti-Jewish campaign, many showed their true colors, full of hate again. And it persists even today, led by the resurrected extreme and chauvinistic ND Party.

In 1991 while I stood in front of the railway station in the village of Gorzkowice, from where my people were likely transported to Treblinka, I tried to analyze my feelings toward the Nazis and their helpers in the murder of millions of Jews. I was searching for words, but couldn't find any that would adequately reflect the incomprehensible, irreconcilable thoughts swirling in my mind. Yes, there were pogroms, massacres, religious strife, and killings before, but never in history had such colossal killing machinery been directed at a defenseless population. Jews were not a nation with their own land to be conquered, nor an occupier of anybody else's territory, nor a people who did harm to the German nation. On the contrary, they made a disproportionately positive economic and cultural contribution to Germany as well as to Poland, Russia, and other nations where they lived.

Absolute madness! How could a small group of insane racists induce millions of their countrymen to participate in such a massive, heinous crime and poison the minds of millions in many countries? Were they all mad? Incomprehensible! Brainwashed by vicious propaganda? Probably! But how could it become so effective in the span of a few years? Maybe the hate was there long before, waiting to be triggered by the racist propaganda? Even so, the decisive role of organization and development of the murder machine belonged to the German Nazis. And the responsibility was theirs. Were they punished enough for their crimes? Does sufficient punishment for such a massive crime exist?

Most of the murderers were not punished. I am a victim since I lost my loved ones. And the pain of my loss does not diminish. Every day I try to put myself in the place of my younger brother Yitzhak or my sisters and parents. I try to imagine how they suffered. When I drink a glass of water, what comes to my mind are the suffocating and thirsty prisoners locked in the boxcars on their way to Treblinka. When I have a meal, I think of starvation in the ghettos and concentration camps. When I go out in the cold, I think of the freezing people standing for hours for the camp roll calls, wearing only those infamous thin, striped clothes. And I wonder whether the consciences of the surviving murderers are tormented, or do they even have a twinge of conscience, or do they laugh as most of them escaped unpunished? The scar is thick but still aches. I have not found a cure.

There is nothing I can do now except grieve. I ask that what Nazi Germany did to the world, not only to Jews, not be forgotten. Tens of millions of people died as a result of their actions. Many nations paid a huge price in human life and material resources to eradicate the vicious Nazi regime. Let us be vigilant and prevent such horror from happening again. Many nations all over the world have pledged: "Never again!" But not all! The danger of another holocaust still exists.

I lost the world of my childhood and I cannot restore it. In that world rich in culture and enterprise, we lost thousands of wonderful scientists, artists, musicians, teachers, artisans, and yes, simple people trying to earn a living by any means available. It was also a loss to the countries of Europe where they resided. And as I thought how I could memorialize my parents and siblings, I decided to share some pictures that are preserved in my head. What follows are portraits I painted of my parents and siblings from memory. In the process of bringing out their faces on paper, I reached a point when I had tears in my eyes. Only then did I feel that my paintings were close to presenting a true likeness. I had one most reliable judge of whether the pictures resemble our loved ones, my older brother Samuel. When Barbara and I visited our relatives in Sydney, Australia, I showed him the portraits, one by one, and he identified each of them. I was satisfied.

Israel ben Shimon Broner, a.k.a. Brauner (1888–Holocaust)

Father was a man of inherent honesty and integrity. He couldn't tell a false-hood, even on the most inconsequential matter. His faith in God was deeply rooted. As a young man he attended Jewish theaters and read Yiddish litera-ture. In his profession as a hat maker, Father exhibited artistic abilities and a meticulous approach to every detail. From 1932, when our family lived in Lodz, I was very close to him, attending prayers together and observing him in his work. This allowed me to appreciate his mild character, his concerns about the entire family, and struggle to provide the means to lead a decent life. Father would have been very proud to know that his two surviving sons placed his name and those of the entire family for eternal memory at the Yad Vashem Holocaust Museum in Jerusalem, the capital of the nation of Israel that carries his name.

Ajdel Ita Broner (1892–Holocaust)

Mother was tall, slender with regular features. Her name, Ajdel, in Yiddish means "gentle." The name fits her character extremely well. I recall her as a content person, despite the hardships that befell our family during the Great Depression. She hoped that more prosperous times would return for us. Unfortunately, this didn't happen, and then the war started. Mother never raised her voice to discipline the children. I cherished her, helped in her work, and loved her deeply. She proudly played the role of mother, wife, housekeeper, and breadwinner. I saw her for the last time, waving goodbye, in November 1939.

Chana Broner-Moszkowicz (1913–Holocaust)

My oldest sister Chana was married and had two small children when the war started. She was very charming and pretty. My memory of her doesn't go far back, since she didn't stay with us in Kamiensk and was not often at home after we returned to Lodz in 1932. The one event that I recall well was her wedding, probably in 1936. I shared with Chana the dreadful days leading to the German occupation of our city.

Her husband, Leib Moszkowicz, was a handsome man whom I liked very much. One day he brought a quarter pound of thinly sliced pineapple to our place. It was a novelty fruit for us, and I still remember its delicious sweet, juicy taste.

I could find no trace of Chana's family after the war.

Esther (1916–Holocaust)

As far back as my memory reaches, Esther was always around. Whether in Kamiensk in the early 1930s or in Lodz until my escape from the occupied city in 1939, I remember her as mother's foremost helper and the children's caretaker. She was intellectually curious, a characteristic that influenced our development. She was a voracious reader of world literature. Esther awakened our curiosity for social and political information as a supplement to our religious upbringing. Learning, working, participating in political life, and being happy under any circumstance were her distinguishing characteristics.

Dvojra (1922–Holocaust)

Dvojra was an enthusiastic and happy teenager. She was tall and pretty with light brown hair and eyes, as was our mother, distinct from the dark coloring of our father and sisters Esther and Shajndl. Until 1939 she attended high school and was a very good student. Dvojra wrote sketches for her school drama group and prepared shows. She exhibited a talent for acting and could have gone far in that direction. War and murder interrupted that beautiful young and very promising life, as it did for so many millions.

Shajndl (1927–Holocaust)

Since Shajndl's was close to me in age, I spent more time with her than with my other sisters. I don't recall her causing any trouble or misbehaving as a child. I think of Shajndl as shy and somewhat introverted. We traveled together to our grandparents in Kamiensk when I was ten years old and Shajndl two years younger. Together, we spent the time as best we could in that little *shtetl*, where there were no attractions of any kind except the Wednesday fair. In November 1939, Shajndl came to replace me in the morning breadline, allowing me to join my older brother Samuel in the escape from German occupation. I always considered this act as a life-saving gift from Shajndl.

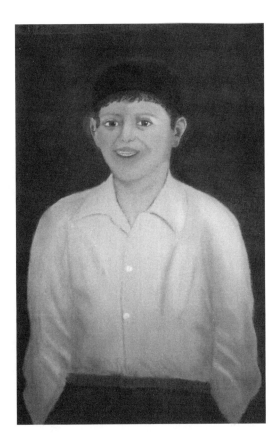

Yitzhak (1930–Holocaust)

The image stored of my youngest brother Yitzhak is seeing him sitting atop the front bed board, solving arithmetic problems. At the age of seven, he already knew the multiplication tables and wanted the older siblings to appreciate his knowledge. I still see us, walking together in the wintertime to school on Jakuba Street, Yitzhak in a warm coat with a fur collar, a gift from our uncle Abraham, the furrier. During the first weeks of German occupation in 1939, we used to get up very early in the morning before the end of the curfew, to get in line for bread. Yitzhak was a smart and joyful boy. Knowing his vitality and character, I am sure that he tried to help the family to get food during the occupation, but for how long?

Historical References

Anders, Wladyslaw. *An Army in Exile.* Nashville, TN: Battery Press, 1981.

Barylski, Robert. *The Soldier in Russian Politics.* New Brunswick, NJ: Transaction Publishers, 1998.

Brent, Jonathan, and Vladimir P. Naumov. *Stalin's Last Crime.* New York: Harper Collins, 2003.

Ciechanowski, Jan M. *The Warsaw Rising of 1944.* Cambridge: Cambridge University Press, 1974.

Davis, Norman. *Rising '44: The Battle for Warsaw.* New York: Viking Penguin, 2004.

Eisler, Jerzy. *Marzec 1968.* Warsaw: Pañstwowe Wydawnictwo Naukowe, 1991.

Gilbert, Martin. *The Second World War: A Complete History.* Revised Edition. New York: Henry Holt and Company, 1991.

Gross, Jan T. *Fear: Anti-Semitism in Poland after Auschwitz: An Essay in Historical Interpretation.* New York: Random House, 2006.

Holocaust Chronicles. Illinois: Publications International, 2000.

Kaczmarek, Kazimierz. *Osmy Bydgoski.* Warsaw: Wydawnictwo Ministerstwa Obrony Narodowej, 1962.

McFaul, Michael. *The End of the Soviet Union: Russia's Unfinished Revolution: Political Change from Gorbachev to Putin.* Ithaca, NY: Cornell University Press, 2002.

Montias, John Michael. *Central Planning in Poland.* New Haven, CT: Yale University Press, 1962.

Rozek, Eward J. *Allied Wartime Diplomacy: A Pattern in Poland.* Boulder, CO: Westview Press, 1989.

Rozenbaum, Wlodzimierz. "The Anti-Zionist Campaign in Poland, June–December 1967," *Intermarium* 1, 3 (1975): 3.

Singer, Isaac Bashevis. *In My Father's Court.* New York: Fawcett Crest, 1966.

Zawodny, J. K. *Nothing but Honour.* Stanford: Hoover Institution Press, 1978.

Index

Pages in italics indicate photographs or illustrations.